TALES FROM THE CITY

Sara Jafari is a British-Iranian author and editor. She has written two novels, *The Mismatch* and *People Change*, both published by Penguin Random House. She was a contributor to the anthologies *Who's Loving You* and *"I Will Not be Erased": Our Stories about Growing Up as People of Colour*. She runs TOKEN Magazine, as well as working as a freelance editor for publishing houses. You can follow her online @sarajafari.

sarajafari.com

Tales from the City

edited by Sara Jafari

TOKEN

Editor & Designer
Sara Jafari

Cover and Interior Illustrator
Raahat Kaduji

Proofreader
Tom MacAndrew

@tokenmagazine
tokenmagazine.co.uk

All writing, images and art included in this issue are the copyright of the authors/artists cited. No part of this publication may be reprinted without permission from the publisher.

ISBN: 9781999825447

For any enquiries contact:
info@tokenmagazine.co.uk.

This anthology has been specially commissioned for Deptford Literature Festival 2023. The festival is produced by Spread the Word and Tom MacAndrew, and is generously supported by Arts Council England.

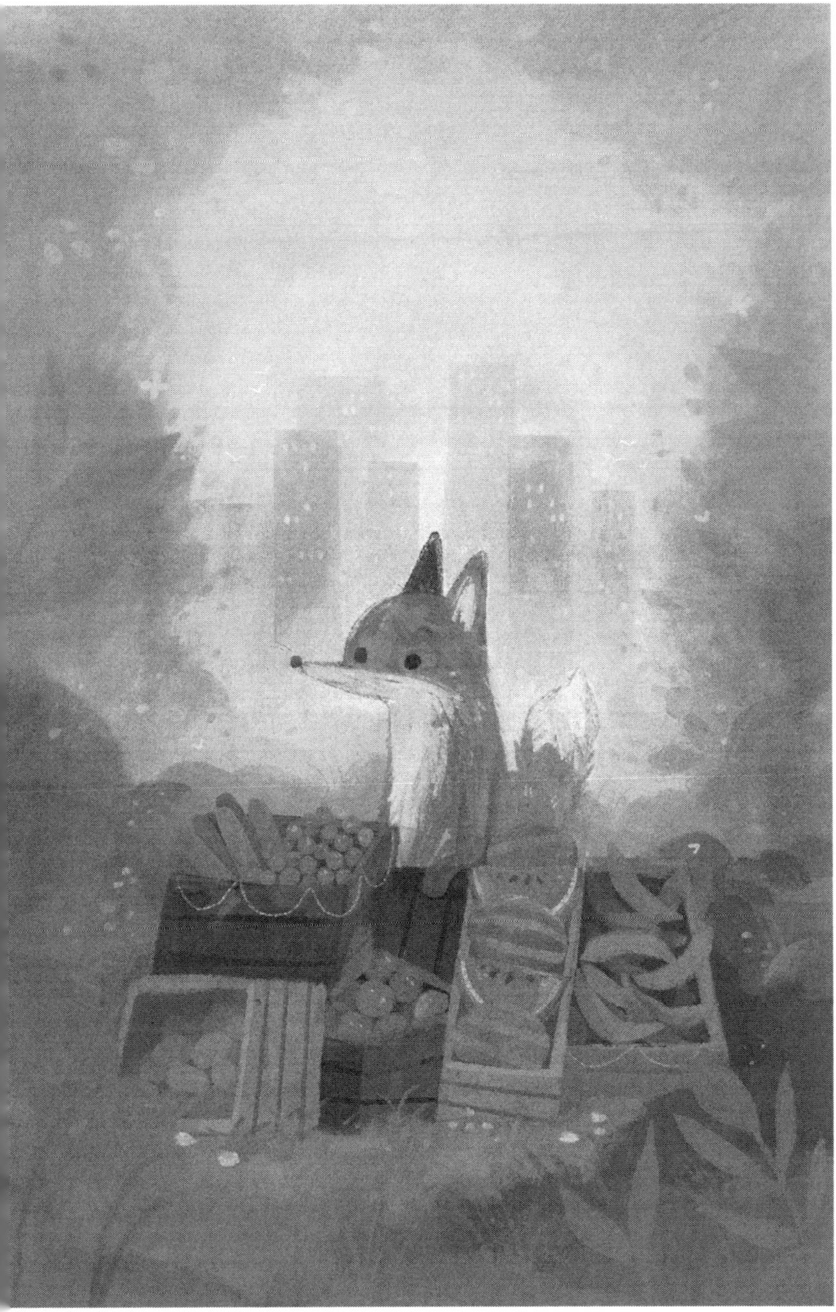

Contents

INTRODUCTION *Sara Jafari*	1
THE HOTTEST DAY *Marie-Claire Amuah*	3
THE STEAMBOAT *Suyin Haynes*	19
TABLE MANNERS *Angel Dahouk*	30
MOONCAKE BOX *Priscilla Yeung*	42
TOFU *Carmen Hoang*	55
WILD WOMEN AND THEIR FRUITS *Kari Pindoria*	63
MARIA AND THE RISING SEA *Anne Elicaño-Shields*	73

FRUITING *Lola Pereira*	81
THE BLUE SHOP *Yuebai Liu*	91
MANGSHO-BHAAT *Santanu Bhattacharya*	100
PROXIMITY *Farhana Khalique*	117
ABOUT THE AUTHORS	129
TOKEN	134
DEPTFORD LITERATURE FESTIVAL	135

Introduction

Welcome to *Tales from the City*, a collection of beautiful short stories and creative non-fiction on food, climate and nature.

This is TOKEN's first anthology. We're an annual print magazine, but we decided to switch it up this year and focus more on longer stories. So, through an open call for submissions by global majority Londoners on the theme food, climate and nature, eleven wonderful pieces were selected. The writers were given the opportunity to approach the theme as literally or as loosely as they wished, and it was fascinating to see the different – and similar – ways each writer approached the theme.

Within the pages of this collection, you will find pieces that are at times heart-breaking but hopeful, at other times humorous and painfully relatable. From an account of a missing person's case during a heatwave (reminiscent to the extreme weather we had in the summer of 2022) to a person experiencing the magic that is making food from their culture for the first time since moving to London, there is so much here to get lost in.

Resounding among almost all the pieces, too, is home and family. It makes sense. Nature, food and climate are essentials for everyone, as are the home (whatever that may look like) and family (whether that be chosen or biological). We see a granddaughter and grandmother reunited, an individual mourning the loss of her parents creating new traditions with her friends, and a comedic snapshot of a family around the dinner table.

I could go on about how wonderful all the pieces are, but I won't. I want you to experience the real breadth and beauty of the pieces within this collection yourself.

I hope you enjoy reading *Tales from the City*.

Sara Jafari

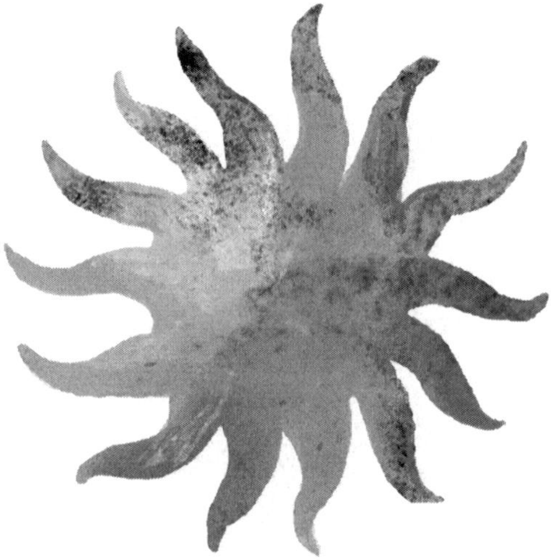

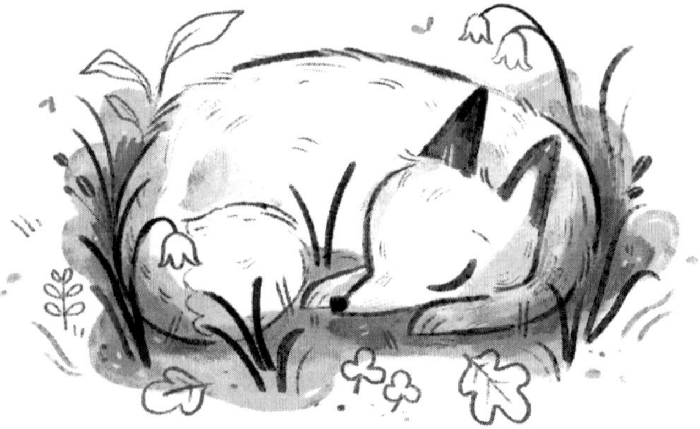

Fiction

THE HOTTEST DAY
Marie-Claire Amuah

It was a summer that had seen highs of 38 degrees in London. 'The hottest summer on record.' Brutal. If someone had said, 'Imagine what it is like to stand under the shade of a sprawling tree under the scorching rays of a 38 degree sun, and inhale,' the imagination would have failed. It was the type of heat you could not imagine – only feel – live – breathe. The type of heat that caused the tarmac footpaths in between the once green parts of the park to crack and reveal an underearth of softened tar that everyday park users were unaware of. It caused people to wonder what you might find if you drilled deep into the grey black ground – or used a digger to chip away at it, piece by piece. It was the type of crack that suggested an earthquake had passed in the middle of the night and the park was the epicentre of it. That it had been so weak in its tremor, residents around the park had neither startled nor stirred at the event or its aftershock. The tar had separated under the unrelenting heat to reveal a depth of ground that the people who walked and played and exercised on its surface had never before known.

Curtains and blinds came down as living rooms took on the heat retaining properties of greenhouses; high rises and lofts became hot as Hades. The heat made long of the nights as people tossed and turned in loose cotton or sweaty nudity in search of comfort. The bats that appeared as darkened shadows against the early evening sky surveyed the stillness of the night. And, just as minds found the temporary relief of sleep, it was dawn once more and the fullness of another stifling day loomed.

When the rain finally came in the last week of September, it reinstated the familiar routine and rhythm of life. Children were able to enjoy the swings and slides without burning their delicate skin and dogs went back to their regular walking times, no longer labouring for breath. Fitness enthusiasts resumed their positions at the outdoor gym and people were able to stand once again in the unshaded centre of the green. The park appeared the same as it always had, but the newly formed cracks in the tarmac remained. They showed that something seismic had occurred in the heat of summer, beyond the dramatic rise in temperature. In the days when the sun seared through the blue sky and distorted the

THE HOTTEST DAY

lightwaves above the ground.

The day the police officers appeared in the park in black patrol boots and neon vests, with compartments for walkie talkies and handcuffs and mace spray, to ask if anyone knew anything about the disappearance of Victoria Summers, users of the park were caught off guard. They were forced around the park's periphery as officers cordoned off its various entrances with the blue and white tape which announced that an incident, perhaps fatal, had occurred in the very centre of the community. They were not privy to the instructions given to the officers to conduct a painstaking search for evidence, for 'anything, no matter how small,' that the investigator informed his officers 'might help to provide leads.' They did not, at that time, know that the body of a twenty-something year old Caucasian female lay in the fields close by, bloodied and bruised, partially clothed. They did not know that the body was that of Victoria Summers.

The community was stirred when her face appeared on posters in and around the park, attached to trees, street lamps and shop windows, under red letters that read 'REWARD'. Mutterings of 'disappearance in suspicious circumstances' and references to 'someone she knew' clashed with expressions that 'no one could ever have imagined something like *this* happening to someone like *her.*' The whisperings in the park competed with the cries of the parakeets, squeals from the children's playground, and gasps from passersby. Police enquiries with local residents returned the same question, 'have you spoken to Mary?'

Mary was the person to talk to. She knew everything about the park and the people who passed through it. Mary knew the park as it was and as it had become. She knew that there was once a time when squirrels were too timid to approach people and that they would now eat monkey nuts from the palm of a stranger's hand. She had seen the stream, once clear and unpolluted, become littered with discarded waste and freeze into an ugly mass at the height of winter. The ice would thaw into something unsightly that she tried hard not to look at. She heard the ducks squeal in distress as they locked webbed feet with food packaging and cigarette butts and other synthetic materials. They had reduced in number over the years. Mary noted the smell that drifted through the windows of the surrounding houses in the hot summer months. It hung in the air with mosquitoes that multiplied aggressively above the stagnant water. She waited for spring to see the daffodils blossom. Every year, she watched and she waited.

It wasn't just that she had seen Vicky's occasional comings and goings; Mary knew when Vicky's door opened, when her curtains twitched and when her music played. She knew when her cat cried at the broken cat flap waiting to be let in through the front door. When that happened it was most likely that Vicky was delayed at work. She would be home before 8pm – unless it was a Thursday and she was out with friends. There was no sign of a boyfriend but there was a love interest who, after some 'here for a fun time not a long time' sightings, seemed like 'a breath of fresh air.' He was, 'a handsome boy, well built.' Mary knew when bikes parked up outside Vicky's door with takeaway deliveries, when she ordered clothes online, which ones and how frequently. She knew when Vicky's recycling indicated an increased intake of alcohol and when her bins overflowed. Mary, voice husky from years of smoking and nicotine coating nicotine on tar coated lungs, recounted this to the police officers who knocked on her door shortly after the body of Victoria Summers had been identified.

Mary had an eyewitness account of the who, the

what, and the where. And in the re-telling of any love story, tragedy or thriller, she was more likely than not to feature as the star witness for the prosecution.

Mary knew that Beatrice was going through a tough time of late. The cancer had ravaged Paul's body and it had become impossible for her to care for him. The crows' feet at the corners of her eyes and accompanying dark circles aged her unfairly but they were testament to the challenges she had been forced to navigate throughout her life. Beatrice had converted her front room into a bedroom when the stairs became too much for Paul to manage. Her back had taken the toll of supporting a body weight three times her own; hoisting and hauling and helping, day in day out. The hospital had given Paul an electric bed so he could raise his head and legs – that helped with the lymphoedema and eased the pressure on Beatrice's long-suffering spine, thank God.

Beatrice had a carer's allowance, of course she did, but looking after Paul was a full-time job. And, before long, the bedsores became too difficult to manage. You had to see Beatrice to understand just how small she was compared to Paul. Anyway, £69.70 every week to care for a sick husband, an agoraphobic son and another who refused to get a job was impossible.

'In the end, he couldn't do a thing for himself. That's why she put him in the hospice. Bowel cancer is what got him in the end.'

Mary had watched from the foot of her doorstep when Justice Hunters knocked on Carol's door and asked to speak to her husband. When Alan appeared on the doorstep in a t-shirt and boxer shorts, a cup of tea in hand, they exposed him as a sexual predator disguised as a reliable plumber and friendly neighbour. Details of the messages he had exchanged with an undercover operative acting as a 14-year-old girl were read out loud and live streamed to a social media site while Mary watched in horror. Her stomach turned on hearing the depraved things he wanted to do to this innocent girl, the pictures and videos he wanted her to send him.

'If he was stunned at being caught, he didn't show it.'

She had watched as Alan attempted a version of events that would have benefited from the words of a police caution, 'you do not have to say anything.'

'He sang like a canary. That was the undoing of him,' she told the police.

By the evening, he was on his way to the coast to live with his mother.

'A 49-year-old man going home to his mother. Can you imagine?'

No one had seen him since.

'People around here won't put up with someone like that.'

Mary told the police about Jim, the local 'dog whisperer' who knew absolutely nothing about dogs but was a self-proclaimed expert. She had forgotten how many times she had seen him remove a lead from the hands of a stranger before forcing their dog onto its side and into submission. He would target new dog owners and speak with such confidence that they would almost always confuse him for someone who knew what he was talking about. This couldn't be further from the truth. Of greater concern to Mary was the wife. Jim struck her as the kind of man who understood his place in life with reference to those beneath him; a man who needed to be in control of a person or a thing, at all times. Whenever she saw them together, the wife would echo Jim's words like a damaged record player. When she was alone, she would barely make eye contact.

'I think she's got "battered wife syndrome", honestly, I do.'

Mary had been in the park when Jim was in charge of a Staffordshire bull terrier that bit off a man's finger in an unprovoked attack. She had watched from a distance, with her shopping bags in hand, as he wrestled to get the dog under control. He screamed the scream of someone who was driving at speed towards a brick wall in a car whose breaks had failed. When he finally did, it was too late; the man lost the index finger on his right hand. To make matters worse, he was a manual labourer. What manual labour he would be able to do with a missing index finger, Mary did not know.

Mary understood that Jim was now defending a claim for damages in the civil courts. She never found out what happened to the dog but it was clear that Jim was at fault. The man had 'delusions of grandeur,' and she had no idea how he could hold himself out as anything other than 'a fraud.'

Mary knew where the seedlings of cannabis plants germinated under fluorescent lighting in well ventilated rooms in and around the park's estate. She knew where the dawn raid for class A drugs and firearms had taken place last week, who was on bail with hidden electronic tags and whose house was under surveillance. She had never been asked to sign any document confirming her status as an official trustee of the Park Association but she referred to herself as 'a non-executive director.'

When the police asked Mary what, if anything, she could tell them about Dennis Marshall at no. 12 across the road, she didn't hesitate.

'Teeth like tombstones.'

Tombstones in an abandoned graveyard that had been forgotten over decades, disfigured by moss and weeds and upturned soil. Surrendered to the elements and a brutalising sun. Teeth in such misalignment you would be forgiven for thinking they were at war with each other. So jagged and criss-crossed that you felt pity for the gum that rooted them. Teeth so yellowed with stains and plaque and god knows what else, that it was natural to wonder if they had ever seen the bristles of a toothbrush. Teeth so truly frightening that a dentist would have wept at the sight of them, laid down tools and conceded defeat. If those teeth were a newborn baby being pushed around by a proud mother in an open pram, and you happened to look inside hoping to glimpse the face of a babbling bundle of joy, you would inhale deeply, take a step backwards and exclaim 'oh my!' at the sight of the gremlin child.

Mary didn't know his name but she had always found him 'odd – suspicious even.' Everyone knew him. If you visited the newsagent, walked through the park or lived in or around the estate, you knew him.

'Well, you knew *of* him,' she corrected. 'If you mention "The Bat Man," everyone will know exactly who you're talking about.'

The Bat Man kept himself to himself. People had tried to speak to him in the past, to greet him in the morning, or hold the door open for him but you would never get a response, not as much as a thank you. And, there was only so much you could do.

He preferred darkness to light and fancied himself a bat watcher. Teeth aside, The Bat Man also had a gangrenous foot. In winter, it would be covered by a sock or bandaged with a flailing dressing. In the summer, it was simply exposed. The Bat Man's foot was 'a horrendous sight' that triggered a gagging reflex if Mary looked at it for too long.

'Absolutely ghastly,' she exclaimed. 'Needless to say, he lives alone. Always has done.'

Pity him though she might, Mary could not bring herself to understand the man's fascination with bat watching. Why he would emerge from a self-imposed isolation every day at sunset, supporting his gait with the use of a walking stick and exposing his foot, nails thickened with fungal infection, to go bat watching. She had seen him with a pair of binoculars around his neck attached to a lanyard. He would go to the park like that. Mary could not imagine what legitimate use a person could have with a pair of binoculars in this area. She could only guess how long he stayed in the park every night, and whether the things he did there were restricted to bat watching, Mary only ever saw him walk to the park, never back home again.

Mary was pleased to be able to assist the officers with their enquiries. On Thursday, she went to the post office with Rita from no. 26 to top up her gas and electricity keys. After that, they went for a coffee and browsed the charity shops before heading home. That's what they did together every Thursday afternoon. Until Rita became poorly with vertigo that is.

'She daren't walk too far now.'

Mary thought – was certain, in fact – that between the hours of 7.15pm and 9pm that evening, she had seen The Bat Man. She was in the recliner in front of the TV for her supper and soaps and had a clear view of Vicky's house across the road through the bay windows. The recliner is where Bob usually sits but he was in the Midlands visiting his brother, Kevin.

'They're 18 months apart, Bob and Kevin, and ever so close. Kevin was recovering from hip replacement surgery and Bob had gone to visit him.'

Mary saw The Bat Man walk past her house which means he would also have walked past Vicky's house.

THE HOTTEST DAY

Certain details stuck in her mind: 'he had one of those nana bags on wheels with him.'

Mary had never seen it before.

'And do you know what he didn't have? His binoculars!'

It was this type of detail that made Mary remember so clearly. It was the type of detail that made her sure.

He would have had no difficulty overpowering someone as slight as Vicky, there was no question about that. Mary had seen The Bat Man knock on Vicky's door which struck her as extraordinary. She had never known him to speak to *anyone* let alone a young girl thirty years his junior. Now, of course, she was able to join the dots together and it made for the most gruesome picture.

'If Bob was home, he would have taken him on.'

Mary could only guess what The Bat Man had inside his bag and how long he had been watching Vicky's comings and goings. She was filled with a powerful regret that she had not gone outside to confront him and ask what business he had with that poor girl.

'Or to let him know that he had been seen. That might have scared him off.'

Mary was so certain of her recollection of events that

identified Dennis Marshall at no. 12 as the last person to see Victoria Summers before her murder that she signed a witness statement to that effect. Come to think about it, she was sure that she had heard a chilling scream – just before 8pm. Mary's blood curdled at the thought of what The Bat Man had done to cause it. Vicky's murder was the type of nightmare suffered by other people in other towns. The kind of story to be reported on the news and not from her doorstep. The murder of a young girl in South London on the hottest day of the year.

It was an impossibly hot day. The kind of heat that scorched the nostrils and the ends of unsightly hairs protruding from the ears of men who had not metrosexualized themselves. An unforgiving heat, 'like an oven.' It crisped the ears of women who wore long hair in trendy top knots or messy buns. It made pale skinned people fearful for the delicacy of their milk white skin. And caused other races to observe the varying shades of brown that melanin could become on people who were already brown. It made the high viz vests of workmen an unbearable layer of protection which it seemed cruel to make them wear. It caused pity for the men outside the South entrance to the park constructing a sturdy frame of scaffolding on top of the pharmacy, barbershop and newsagents. It forced bus drivers whose routes circled the park's border to strip down to their vests in stifling cabins. It caused dog walkers to change their routines to walk at dawn and after sunset, testing the heat of the ground with the backs of their hands before allowing the paws of their beloved canines to make contact. It singed the grass from a juicy green to a dehydrated straw-like colour. It made of the children's swings and slides a scorching hazard, metal upon which a raw egg could fry. It slowed the pace of all pedestrians everywhere. It made people long for rain.

The heat of that day caused people to stay in their homes, windows and curtains drawn, craving relief from the heat. The whirl of fans, inadequate against the stifling air, hummed throughout houses in which complaints of the unbearable heat echoed. It was unlike any heat Mary had ever known. A heat that suspended life and dispensed with habit and routine. She should have seen Vicky's front door. Had she not been oppressed by the intolerable heat that held her hostage at home in her bra and briefs. Mary could have seen Vicky's front door. Had she not closed her curtains against the scorching sun before it announced itself in an unfamiliar sky that morning. Had she opened them when the moon finally appeared in the late evening sky and before she settled in the recliner for the evening. The one that Bob used to sit in before he died: Bob's favourite chair. Her beloved Bob. But the evening was as sweltering as the day was unbearable. Mary would have seen Vicky's front door had the heat not caused her to surrender to a fatigue that claimed her appetite before she had even tasted her supper that evening. Had she been awake. Had confusion not come in the night like a thief to steal her well-intentioned mind from her sleeping body – and settled there. A confusion that had come in recent months to colour the present and interfere with her recollection of the past. She would have known that the bats that appeared as darkened shadows against the early evening sky flew unseen amongst the trees in the park that evening.

The summers had been getting hotter, year on year. Mary had seen them come and go.

Fiction

THE STEAMBOAT
Suyin Haynes

She didn't really want to host the reunion dinner. For one thing, it wasn't even her idea. It was Eve who had suggested that everyone get together for the occasion. The emoji-filled responses and their subtext in the group chat betrayed the real reason they were gathering at her new place: to distract her from the inevitable emotions that would arise this time of year. She understood, and yielded to their enthusiasm.

Lifting the thin slices of marbled beef out of their polystyrene foam packaging, she started peeling back the clingfilm slowly from the red and white flesh. She laid them out on the porcelain plate, one strip alongside another strip, alongside another strip. It wouldn't be long now until her guests started arriving. She had prepared a script in her head, just in case: how to explain the different components of the dinner to unfamiliar palates, how it was perfectly hygienic to cook meat this way, how she had no idea whether the fish balls actually contained fish – only that they tasted good.

Above the sink, the cold January rain left droplets on the window, each encircled by misty condensation that radiated from the activity in her kitchen. There was a slight crack between the bottom and the top panes, which didn't quite fit seamlessly together, leaving a draught imperceptible to visitors. It was noticeable, though, if you were the flat's sole inhabitant, spending your first winter there.

Slicing tofu, she saw the tiny imprints the knife's metal made in the chopping board with each cut. The tofu was firm; it needed to be, so that it could carry the flavouring of the stock. She feared using the silken kind could risk disintegrating, causing a mess – both to eat and to apologise for. She wasn't used to cutting firm tofu though, applying more pressure than needed. Each cut landed against the grain of the wood, creating a criss-cross imprint of perpendicular lines. She tried to remember whether her mother's chopping board carried the same patterns of dinners gone by. It was one of the many items she'd said goodbye to when she cleared out the house. Its presence in a different kitchen would have felt wrong.

She paused, noticing a spider crawling along the skirting board. Its spindly legs moved quickly, straddling the horizontal ledge. The drop down to the floor seemed so vast. Her father used to point out the spiders' webs, splayed out as if someone had thrown them across the gravestones of Nunhead Cemetery, or woven between the craggy ruins of colossal dead tree trunks lying on their sides in the woods of Beckenham Place Park. Both places became unexpected havens for them during the first months of the pandemic, before he was no longer able to go outside. Both, in their own strange ways, acted as pockets of peace, never properly explored by parent nor child before, until circumstances forced them to seek new air and space where they could nearby.

'Spider's web strong like steel, you know,' he'd say – yet another unsubstantiated fact, an old snippet of hearsay like the many scattered through their conversations over her lifetime. The first time, she'd challenged him. As he repeated it during their final walks together, she nodded in agreement. His mind was now in a place where moments later, he'd forget that he'd ever said the statement at all.

She looked back again, and the spider was gone.

Cardboard boxes were still unopened and unpacked in the kitchen-dining room. She hadn't had time to arrange things properly yet, so a various assortment of Lao Gan Ma jars and Lee Kum Kee bottles stood on the marbled countertop forlornly, judging her for not yet putting them on their rightful shelves in the magnolia-coloured cabinets. These condiments had been hallmarks of her childhood. The ones she now owned had congealed remnants of sauce around the plastic cap, and drippings of red oil leaving a discoloured trail of straight lines down the label.

She started peeling the outer slightly limp leaves of the bok choy away, and ripping the fresher inner leaves apart from the base. It had just been easier to buy the vegetables from Longdan, the local Asian food supermarket – even if it meant the produce wasn't quite as fresh or cheap as she'd been used to living back at home.

Their go-to supermarket was Wing Yip. Usually, the three of them would trundle onto the 119 bus with their bags for life, twisting and turning through Hayes and Shirley, racing the trams through Croydon, before stopping at the green-scaled, pagoda-style gate of the supermarket/shopping centre/restaurant complex. You had to wear layers to go in, even in the summer, as the temperature of the cavernous warehouse was always kept well below 15 degrees. Her mum would remind them to bring their 'jill-etts' in their bags, ending the word with a hard 't'.

Preparing for the steamboat was a mid-January ritual – one she had to do alone this time, declining Cleo's offer to come over early to help. It was something her parents had done since they met in

THE STEAMBOAT

1990, a few years after they both arrived in London – her dad from Hong Kong, her mum from Ipoh. Neither had been back since, nor had she ever visited. Painful memories lay in both places for both parents, and as the years went by, she learned not to enquire, for they had buried their pasts so deep they had become irretrievable.

While her classmates talked about the Christmas dinners they couldn't wait for as early as the first day of November, she quietly looked forward to January all year long. That was the time of celebration and indulgence in their house, when her parents would buy enough food for at least eight, even though they were only three.

On these mammoth trips to Wing Yip, they'd debate over which meat to cook, which fish looked fresher, which kind of noodle they wanted in the broth, and how much they'd physically be able to carry home on the bus with six arms between them. Freezers filled with pre-made dim sum, char siu bao, and crispy salt and pepper squid lined the aisles, and shoppers' trolleys were laden high with 10kg bags of rice, bumper boxes of eggs and bundles of oranges, stem and green leaf still intact.

As a child, she'd point out and pick up random items – grape-flavoured boiled sweets, packets of seaweed strips, Vitasoy cartons – captivated by their colourful packaging, placing them in the trolley surreptitiously (or so she thought). Her mum would try to get her as excited about the food she had grown up eating back home in Malaysia: bean curd skin, lotus root, winter melon, enoki mushrooms with their slender stems and pearly bulbous heads. Now as an adult, she appreciated these foods much more than those wrapped in plastic artifice; each bite a taste of a home she'd never known, 10,000 kilometres away.

Her last task was to make the wontons. She'd already prepped the filling in the morning, enough for twenty parcels – and was relieved that the guest list tonight was a carnivorous one. She lifted the bowl out of the fridge – a gelatinous mix of minced pork and chopped spring onion, seasoned with dashes of salt, pepper, soy sauce and sesame oil, bound together by a beaten egg. Using her thumb and index finger, she shaped a scoop of the filling into a small ball, placing it in the centre of the square wonton wrapper, which had a fine layer of powder on it. Once submerged in the steamboat's boiling water, the pastry would soften, cook and shrink around the meat it housed, creating an effect her dad always said looked like brains.

She dabbed water round the edges of the pastry sheet and folded it over the filling into a triangle. How did she know what to do, how big the filling should be? It was instinctual, muscle memory; imprinted on her brain from years of watching her mother's nimble fingers mould the meat, then fold the pastry. Mould, then fold, then mould again. 'Simpler this way,' her mum would say. 'Can't be bothered with all this faffing and fanciful making shapes.' She stood back, admiring her handiwork – twenty, near identical, off-yellow triangles, all lying on top of one another to make a lopsided pyramid on the plate.

The components of the steamboat were really very simple, and required minimal prep. But she did have to admit, it looked impressive as she laid the table for six. Plates piled with all hers and her parents' favourites, ready to be shared. The crowning glory was the steamboat itself. Whereas the chopping board would have been a daily reminder of her parents' absence, she reasoned that their steamboat and its metallic curves would be a sharp moment of pain, over quickly: taken out once a year, then washed, dried, and repackaged back into its box, not to emerge again until the next Lunar New Year. She rinsed it clean, put it at the centre of the table and then filled it up with stock that had been simmering away on a low heat.

She last did this routine exactly a year ago, when it was only her and her mother eating – a reunion dinner for two. Although her mother was physically there, she had been absent since her father had passed on to the next life the previous December. The last months together were hard on all of them, as his condition grew progressively worse. He no longer recognised them, and they no longer recognised the man who brought the loud belly laughs, the fantastical folk stories, the humour and lightness, to their trio. Christmas was spent in the hospice, and New Year's Day accepting that the inevitable had happened.

Three months after that last reunion dinner, in April, her mother joined him. 'I can't believe it, it's so sudden. I'm so sorry,' Heather replied when she told the group, in a message she had typed, erased and re-typed so many times, because pressing the green arrow to send would make it actually true. It was a benign statement of condolence, but she frowned, turning her phone to airplane mode. Didn't Heather know that it wasn't sudden at all? That part of her mother had died when her father did? After that exchange, she remained in airplane mode for quite some time.

The buzzer from downstairs went off. She picked up the white plastic phone – another feature of the flat that felt slightly alien – balancing it between her ear and her shoulder, holding down the handset's button with her right thumb, listening to the cheery chatter rattling over the intercom. It would take about five minutes for whoever had just arrived to climb up the flights of stairs, although that could be up to seven minutes if Alex was in the first delegation, knowing how he would likely stop to marvel at the most ordinary of stairwells.

Five minutes of breathing time before the evening began. Before she shared a tradition from a past she so often yearned for a deeper connection to, with friends who were yearning to rebuild a connection with her. She traced her finger round the circumference of the jade pendant hanging round her neck. It had been her por-por's until she passed. Then, it had become her mother's. Now, it was hers.

She opened the door, and was surprised to see everyone had arrived together, coming up the last flight of stairs, red-cheeked and ready to eat. Eve was at the front of the group, bundled up in a characteristically arresting neon blue fur coat (fake) and knitted balaclava. She heard her mum's voice, as she had commented so many times on Eve's fashion choices: 'Aiya, another one of those crazy outfits!' Micah was next, still defrosting their hands from the cold outside, followed by Heather and Alex, bearing respectively a bunch of eucalyptus and a bottle of her favourite wine (available at any decent newsagents). And lastly there was Cleo, who had foregone her family's own reunion dinner this evening to be there, for her.

Words of welcome escaped her briefly, before she remembered that she was the host – although the flat she was inviting them into still didn't quite feel like her home. Eve, being Eve, leapt towards her. 'It's so good to see you,' she said, hugging her close. One by one, they embraced her, ears bumping, necks nestling, hair smelling – unfamiliar sensations she hadn't experienced in months. Whispered 'I missed you's turned into gasps of wonder as they walked straight into the dining room and saw the table, the steamboat lying majestic at its centre.

Once everyone settled, space at the table was tight. After all, she didn't expect she'd be regularly hosting six people in the flat. There was just enough room for elbows, for an arm to reach over another without it getting too uncomfortable – and besides, they were all familiar enough to do this by now. Over the years, the six of them had seen each other at their bests and their worsts – apart from her, over the last eight months. She hadn't wanted anyone, not even those she trusted most, to perceive her in her grief, to be privy to any part of the agony that her losses had wrought, even if it was as an observer.

The steamboat bubbled a little, making its presence heard. Micah sat next to her, resting a hand gently on hers. 'Thank you, for having us, for doing all of this,' they said, gesturing with the other hand to the table crammed with food; everything she had sliced, chopped and laid out to be boiled, scallion greens to be sprinkled, soy sauce and chilli oil to be garnished. 'Tonight feels really special.'

She looked down at their fingers, now loosely intertwined, months of messages unanswered in their tender touch. 'Thank you for coming, and for asking me to do this,' she said, not looking up. As her gaze trained downwards, her brimming tears stinging her lower lash line, she thought she saw the spider reappear, scuttling back along the skirting board into the kitchen.

She stood up, picking up the handle of the ladle. 'Now, lái. Let's eat.'

Fiction

TABLE MANNERS
Angel Dahouk

'I was upstairs, in the bedroom upstairs, you know,' Mum begins. 'And I look out the window. I see a cat. He was trying to cross the road.'

She pushes ratatouille, potatoes and grilled lamb onto any unguarded plate.

'And the cat, he wait. The road was very busy, a lot of cars. I don't know where all these people go.'

Odhran listens and nods as he politely shields his plate from the serving spoon. I warn him every time to skip breakfast before lunch at my parents'.

'That all you eat?' she scolds my husband. 'You too thin, you should eat more.'

My father, at the head of the table, sits silently. He watches Mum closely, drawing audible breaths when drops of wine meet the tablecloth as she pours.

'You like your lunch?' she enquires before the food has reached a mouth.

Odhran swiftly stows away a spoonful, widens his eyes and makes animated sounds as he chews.

Mum looks pleased.

'Good, you enjoy!' she says as she edges around the table, checking to see what has been overlooked.

'The cat,' she continues. 'He want to cross the road.' She is straining with the gravy boat now, holding it out to my husband who is landlocked between the patio door and me. 'He did very well, he look out for cars, both ways, you know? Move your plate here, son.'

For almost forty years, the dining room has remained unchanged. Despite the large patio door that dominates the far wall, the room always sits in shadow behind full-length net curtains. A stiff sofa occupies one corner, a cast-off from the Connaught Hotel where my father worked. He retired almost twenty years ago. On the opposite side of the room, a dark-stained cabinet displaying untouched crystalware looms over the dining table. Anchored to the wall, a pair of Victorian-style lamps that are rarely switched on. Mum adds her religious wall art and porcelain figurines to the various side-tables that cripple any chance of flow through the room. Everything has its place, including me.

'Sit here in your chair,' Mum chirrups each time I visit, gesturing toward my corner of the dining table. Now she takes her seat across from me and lowers her eyes, delivering her thank yous to *deus* even though everyone is already eating. She taps her forehead, stomach, left shoulder, right shoulder, before lifting her head.

'When the cars, they stop, he cross the road, the cat.' Mum laughs, picks up her fork and waves it at Odhran. 'Can you believe? He cross the road, you know? He sit near to the tree on the other side. He make it fine, he still alive!'

'So, how is your family, Odhran?' my father asks. He nods at my husband's response, reaching for his glass of wine, not really absorbing anything Odhran is telling him. The conversation dies quickly.

As the silence lengthens, Odhran turns his attention away from my father to the three glasses in front of him, one with red wine, one with white, and one containing the remains of a Guinness. My father likes to have a pint of Guinness poured and waiting for when Odhran arrives. As he drinks, my father will share stories of his travels around Ireland. He once casually mentioned that he was invited to be a linesman at Croke Park. The image of my petite, tanned father in shorts, running a flag up and down the sidelines, had my husband and I in giggles.

'Have you spoken to your sister recently?' my father asks me.

'We emailed a couple of weeks ago,' I tell him. 'But she hasn't been in touch since the scan.'

TABLE MANNERS

Mum sneers and shakes her head. 'She silly, your sister, always talking about her cats. She call me the grandmother of cats. You must be joking! I love the cats. They very intelligent creatures, very intelligent, the cats. But I am not a grandmother of cats! She will be sorry when she gets old and she alone.'

'Never mind your sister,' my father says firmly. 'She has chosen her path. You concentrate on your own life.'

The television, only recently updated to flatscreen, is murmuring in the corner of the room while we eat. An advert appears announcing that this Wednesday's lottery is a rollover. Mum begins fidgeting and tutting.

'I see people scratching the cards and throw them in the bin. Win nothing. Ha!' She blows air through her nostrils. 'Stealing people in broad daylight. Crooks. They are thieves. Stealing people. Don't you think, Odhran? I am right?'

Beneath the flatscreen sits a digital box. Every fifteen minutes, the box whirrs for sixty seconds before quietening down again. My parents are unbothered, but Odhran looks questioningly at the box, then at me. I shrug and shake my head.

'Farrad, do you know why your digital box makes that sound?' Odhran ventures. 'Is it overheating, do you think?'

'Odhran, I tell you what the problem is. The man

who sold it to me is very clever. He is from the Czech Republic.'

'A friend of yours?' asks Odhran.

'No, no. He came by recommendation, you know, from a friend. Anyway, he comes here to fit the box and to add the channels I want to watch – all my Arabic channels.' My father reaches for the remote control and squints at the buttons. After some deliberation, he selects one, pointing the remote at the television, and frowning with impatience. A dialogue box eventually appears.

'Ah! You see' he begins as he scrolls through Al Jadeed, Al Jazeera and Al-Manar. 'This is why I have the box. But he is very clever, the Czech. He has put something in the machine that sends him signals, tells him what I'm watching. Then, he removes my favourite channels. They just disappear one day, gone! So I have to phone him and pay him to come here and install them again.'

As my father is speaking, Mum picks up a nearby serving bowl, too small for the volume of food it contains.

'Here, try this.' She holds the bowl over Odhran's plate. 'Spinach with pine nuts. Make you strong, like Popeye.' She explodes with laughter as she transfers one, two, three spoonfuls. Odhran looks despairingly at his plate where the spinach now swamps the lamb and potatoes.

'It's okay,' I remind him. 'You don't have to finish everything. Just eat what you can.' He has become accustomed to my parents' aggressive hospitality, but still cannot successfully fend off the extras. An offering has to be firmly rejected three times before my parents retreat.

When we were children, Mum would sit across the table from my sister and I with a wooden spoon in front of her. If we told her we were finished before the plate was empty, she would raise the wooden spoon threateningly. Sometimes, I wasn't able to hold it all down. For Mum, this somehow seemed the better option than leaving food on the plate.

Despite beginning last, Mum's plate empties first. Her eye is hovering impatiently over the other plates.

'And work?' my father questions Odhran again. 'Is your work going well?' He breaks a piece of bread as my husband explains that work has been busy.

'Well, you have responsibilities now,' my father responds. 'No messing around anymore. I worked very hard for my daughters.'

Odhran nods in agreement and continues to eat, allowing my father to revel in his own achievements.

'I work hard too.' Mum is frowning. 'I wash, I clean, I cook.'

My father raises his head sharply and glares at my

mother.

'Why you look at me that way?' she exclaims as she starts piling crockery, leaning over to retrieve a dropped fork, bringing it crashing down on an angled plate. 'You always say these things, you are wrong. Behave yourself, Farrad.'

'Who put food on the table?' my father asks pointedly. 'Who took the girls to and from school? Who took them to ballet, even to piano lessons, on the weekend? Who bought them everything they asked for?'

Mum's face is flushed. She winces down the last of her wine and begins a broken tirade, veering from English into Portuguese. It continues as she carries plates into the kitchen. She turns the tap on and raises her voice so we can still hear what she has to say over the rush of water. 'Always blame me. *Não faz mal.*' She breathes out heavily. 'Never can do right. *Espirito de contradição*. God forgive him.'

I push back my chair, barely standing before my father rests his hand on mine, signalling to leave it be. Odhran reaches for the breadbasket as I try to get the conversation going again.

'What's happening in Lebanon, Dad? Do you think we'll have a chance to go out there before the end of the year?' I ask.

My father looks down at the table and shakes his

head.

'The situation is very bad, *habibti*, very bad. You know they still haven't elected a President? There is rubbish on the streets, no government to take it away. People, they cannot breathe. It is looking very, very bad. There will be trouble again, believe you me.'

I catch Odhran's eye. We both silently acknowledge that this is the response we were expecting. My father spends hours each day watching his Arabic news channels and drawing conclusions that I can never counter.

Mum enters the room again, still furious.

'Mum, how is Aunty Adriana?' I ask.

A deep grunting sound emerges from my father. Mum doesn't seem to hear and smiles.

'She send a kiss. *Beijo.*'

Mum comes round to my side of the table, takes the glass of sparkling water from my hand, and leans down to kiss me on each cheek. Pulling back, she places my drink down on the table, and chuckles.

'She laugh, Adriana – I tell her the story of the cat, how he cross the road, very clever.' She claps her hands together, and heaves with laughter.

My father watches as she stands over the table, clutching at the edges. She exhales laughter, it comes out in swoops and phews so that her eyes tighten and her cheeks expand with colour. My father turns to my husband.

'I am sorry, Odhran, the service is very slow here.'

Mum's laugh is cut short. 'What you mean the service is slow?'

My father looks at Mum once again but doesn't say a word. She lets it go this time and turns her attention back to me.

'Adriana, she went to Monte. Remember Monte? You been. It's beautiful, full of food. You know, they celebrate food.'

'Yes, the food festival,' I encourage her. 'I've heard about…' She doesn't let me finish.

'You remember your father, what he did in Monte, you remember?' Her voice is rising. 'In the car, you remember?' She is stifling inevitable laughter.

'Yes, Mum. He knocked a car mirror as he was driving.' She has already released the laughter. It soars sharply before levelling out.

My father doesn't take his eyes off her. His tone is flat. 'And you remember what you called me?'

This story is repeated around the dinner table at least once every nine months. I was about thirteen at the time. Monte is a village nestled high in the hills overlooking Funchal, the capital city of Madeira. My father was muttering behind the wheel of a rental car, still thrown by right-hand driving even after a week. He had quickly lost his nerve with the narrow cliff roads, yelling at his family to please let him concentrate. The radio was switched off and the windows wound up. My sister and I made ourselves small in the backseat, facing away from each other and out separate windows, trying to ignore the heat and our father's low-toned frustration at the closely parked cars either side of the road.

Moving forward slowly, a line of vehicles mounting behind us, the car suddenly jolted down on one side as it rolled into a pothole. Our car mirror collided with a parked car, creating an enormous whipping sound. Mum, startled by the break in silence, released her shock by yelling, 'Stupid MAN!' Over twenty years later, my father still hasn't forgotten or forgiven.

'Stupid MAN!' I impersonate Mum, and everyone around the table laughs, even my father. I gently lay a hand on Odhran's knee and quietly add, 'He always laughs when I mimic Mum.'

'Even the cat,' Mum says between giggles. 'He is more careful than your father!'

'What – did he make it back to the other side?' my father asks.

'What you talking about?' Mum clatters with laughter. Odhran is laughing along with her. She turns to him with tears in her eyes. 'What he talking about? Do you know?' They laugh together some more.

My father looks from my mum to me, and makes

a 'she's loopy' sign with his finger. He pushes his chair back and heads to the fridge for another bottle of wine.

'Ah!' Mum exclaims as the opening riffs of the BBC snooker theme tune filters out from the television. She raises her arms and clasps her hands in a victory pose above her head. 'Yes, Ronnie! You like Ronnie, Odhran? Ronnie O'Sullivan?'

My husband shrugs.

'He very good,' Mum says.

My father retakes his seat, pours himself a glass of wine, and refills one of Odhran's three glasses, before setting down the bottle. Mum's glass is empty.

Odhran begins an anecdote about Alex Higgins – how, toward the end of his life, he used to play pool around the pubs in Belfast for beer money. 'He would drink every night in Lavery's. He used to dress in black, always wore a hat and he had this taut white face, really haunting. He could barely speak after the operation on his throat. They say that he threatened to set the UVF on Dennis Taylor after a…'

'Yes. Very good. Ha!' Mum calls out loudly as Ronnie sinks the first red. 'I make a cake, Odhran, you want to try?'

Odhran nods, giving up on his story.

'Good boy,' Mum says. 'You should eat more.' She is standing, but is going nowhere.

TABLE MANNERS

'Everybody happy?' she asks.

No one replies.

'Good. Everybody happy. That's the main thing.'

Fiction

MOONCAKE BOX
Priscilla Yeung

As the plane descended, I held the metal box tighter. The paint on the edges had faded, and the surfaces were rough and battered over time. The contents inside rattled as the aircraft broke through the final layer of clouds. I could hear the sound of the air flowing fast, or maybe it was just the engine. Passengers looked out from the window, and the concrete jungle below loomed larger and larger.

I felt claustrophobic just looking down from above at my former home. There were so many buildings. They took over the mountains and the sea. The buildings were too high. Nature was struggling through the veins of the concrete. There were too many people to accommodate – close to eight million in a city a sixth of the size of London.

The landing was smooth. 'Welcome to the Hong Kong International Airport,' announced the captain in his soothing London accent. I would like to stay in his voice and not move ahead. I didn't like what the future held.

Notifications on my phone exploded after the twelve-hour flight, and among them were four snappy texts from my mum:

Welcome back.
No time to freshen up.
Taxi's waiting.
We'll go straight to Grandma's.

Twenty minutes later, my mum and I met. We hugged. She ushered me out. 'Go go go,' she said. This felt right. People were always rushing in this city.

I told you that I didn't like what the future held.

As soon as we left the airport, the noise, pollution and hot air attacked me. I didn't sit well with them. I missed my home already, my humble abode in the green part of Lewisham. It was busy, Lewisham, but never as suffocating as it could get in Hong Kong.

The taxi was quick, spinning at a hundred and twenty kilometres per hour on the motorway, but still it couldn't get rid of the never-ending wall of homes on my left. Ten buildings stuck together with no gaps between them. They called the little squares on each floor apartments. The size of a shoe box, or a coffin to be more realistic. Like a Jenga tower, many Jenga towers.

We arrived at the hectic care home, pastel pink, nurses in white, too warm for stockings. The air smelt like sanitiser. The air-conditioning blew out cool recycled air and a loud hum. My bulky suitcases were in the way. The carers 'tsk'-ed as they walked past, pushing moaning old women in wheelchairs. Their eyes had lost colour as if their souls were stolen by time and sickness.

Someone fired, 'You have terrible massage skills! I'm in more pain than before. You're getting it all wrong. You shouldn't be working here!' The piercing high pitch alone could be a torture weapon. No one seemed to be alarmed by this except me, gasping. How rude! Mum gave me an I-have-warned-you-already face, and our footsteps followed the swearing. She told me before, when we were on FaceTime, that Grandma throwing a tantrum had become a daily routine.

'That's Grandma?' I mouthed back, too shocked to make a sound.

Bullshit. But my mum took me to her ward, and my grandma's name was tagged to her bed.

Nothing about this wicked old lady resembled my beloved grandma. I wrapped my arms around the metal box and hugged it closer to my chest. The Grandma I knew was in there, and I mustn't let this hot-tempered, mean witch steal my fond memories.

'Siu-Ping is back from England, look!' my mum held her hand, drew her attention, spoke loudly and pointed at me. Her zoomed-out gaze returned, focused on me, and then looked away.

'You traitor!' She gave me a side glance and shouted from her chest, which made her cough violently. Her pitch was high as if her vocal cords were stretched too thinly and would snap at any moment.

'How dare you leave Hong Kong and move abroad? You are not my granddaughter anymore.'

Mum fed her water with a straw, and she complained, 'Are you daft? The water is too hot! My tongue's burning!'

It felt like I had just flushed a thousand pounds down the drain for this stupid plane ticket. I had paid to get told off by this whiny crone that couldn't possibly be my grandma. My lovely, elegant grandma with quiet strength and composure that most men couldn't compare.

Until half of her body was paralysed from a stroke – a stroke from a bad fall at my mum's home.

There was nothing but aggravation in her eyes, and her face was lopsided and drooling. The near-fatal fall two years ago had done something to her nerves. Her personality had switched from kind to harsh, sweet to bitter, forgiving to resentful, as if the world owed her millions. She would no longer be herself again. Until her death.

And when would that be?

I knew about all this. My mum moaned to me over FaceTime every week, but the reality hadn't kicked in until now. Grandparents are not supposed to change. They always look the same since we were born. Old and kind, like the Queen. The grey hair, the wrinkles, the clothes that stay the same. They make the same dishes, and their homes never get a renovation. They stand the test of time – an unchanging force, the foundation of their grandchildren's upbringing. Security.

'Come and sit next to Grandma,' my mum dragged and forced my butt on the orange plastic chair. We were on her good side, but she looked frail and tiny as a child. There was no fat but only flappy skin dangling around her bones and sulking hollows below her cheeks. Green veins crawled up her neck like a tree, like Yoda. So many veins. The veins on her thin white arms were vomit-green, popping out under her papery skin.

'What's that?' she stared at the metal box on my lap.

The blue lid read 'Wing Wah Mooncake' in red

MOONCAKE BOX

Chinese brush strokes and an illustration of a full yellow moon and two pink peonies. Everyone in Hong Kong used to gift these cakes to family and friends during the mid-autumn festival. Four cakes in a tin. They could be square or round. A whole salted egg yolk was wrapped in the middle by a brown paste made with lotus seeds, lard and sugar. As with everything Chinese, the cake was meant to be shared. I could never manage more than a quarter of a mooncake, and it was always washed down with a strong brew of jasmine tea and the sourness of a pomelo. It was the density that took my appetite away. What I enjoyed much more was to keep the box and store my childhood treasures in it. A Barbie doll, random medals, and a stack of letters. Some people even put cash, stocks and bond certificates in them, before these were all digitised. Grandma and I used to be pen pals, starting when I was still in Hong Kong, before my memory was solid. She'd post me pink Hallmark cards with a teddy bear on the cover, sometimes two, and her long message would take over the entire inside of the card, sometimes even spilling onto the back. Her handwriting was calligraphy-like, even with the cheapest ballpoint pen, but it was difficult to understand because she used poetic words and elegant prose.

I opened the box, picked out my favourite card and immediately shut the lid. It had a simple pastel blue front with two bears hugging each other, and the message said: 'For someone special, best of luck!'

'You posted me this when I was about to move to England.' I avoided looking at her and started reading it aloud, just in case she shouted again.

Dear Siu-Ping,

You're going to England for university, and Grandma is very proud of you. You remember Grandpa was a sailor, and he used to travel to Europe too. England will be very cold, even in September, so make sure you layer up. Take the sterling notes in this envelope and get a hot drink when the weather gets rough. Remember to call your mother from time to time. She'll miss you like I missed your grandpa back in the day, but I'll miss you in a million more ways.

Love, Grandma

My voice softened. Her generation was people of few words. She never said I love you with her mouth, but on paper, her affection overflowed. I could feel it even when I was reading it now, twenty years later.

I looked up. Mum had tears in her eyes, but Grandma just stared at the ceiling. The light was cold, white and harsh. It seemed like the ceiling was more interesting than me. She really had lost it, I thought. She didn't care or remember anymore.

Then suddenly, she came back from her zone and demanded, 'Read another one.'

I picked another one, then another one. I giggled when she wrote something funny, but she didn't. She listened, eyes fixated on the roof, with no comment. I didn't hold her hand. I didn't move the chair any closer. I read and read, feeling the dryness in my mouth, but I kept going. My fingers just clenched onto the box, and I read until the nurse said visiting time was over.

I duly stood up and took a last, or maybe it was the first, proper look at her. I mean a real look at her. The purple veins under her eyes, the cloudy pupils, the jade bracelet dangling loose on her wrist. She didn't say goodbye, just asked us to roll her body to face the television.

That night I couldn't sleep. And it wasn't jet lag.

I walked around my family's apartment and was surprised to hear cicadas were still chirping. The little airborne insects just hid in the trees and sang all summer long, never to be seen, and usually died before autumn came. They were so loud that the traffic became distant. They muted the city – my home, I guess.

I brewed some jasmine tea and sat by the window. Eight lines of cars were roaming through the super highway, even at this hour. Some flats in those Jenga towers still had their lights on – probably students burning their midnight oil. It was too much. The full moon hung proudly in the sky, getting ready for the mid-autumn festival. My mum didn't eat mooncakes anymore. It was bad for her cholesterol. Everyone's getting old.

I picked out one specific card buried at the bottom of the box. This was the very last one my grandma wrote to me, only because I never wrote back.

Dear Siu-Ping,

It seems like you'll be settling down in England for good. I'll miss you, but I understand. We are all well in Hong Kong. Every morning I go for a walk with Grandpa. He has dementia now and thinks he's in Europe, sailing like he was in his twenties. After our walk, I'll go home and read your letters over and over again from when you were nine to when you graduated. Your handwriting has changed so much, but it's always full of strength and determination. You can tell a lot from penmanship.

You don't write to me anymore. I understand, and I don't blame you. Take care in London, and make sure you are warm enough. I know you don't need this anymore, but I've put a few sterling notes in this letter anyway. Use the money to get a hot drink.

Love, Grandma

Why did I stop writing to Grandma? My last letter was almost ten years ago. I knew why and I was ashamed of it. I rejected my Chinese identity because living as a foreigner in London was so hard, and my grandma's words reminded me exactly of that – that I was a foreigner. I didn't want to be one. It was easier to keep my memories and roots tucked away in a box.

Maybe Grandma understood, or perhaps she didn't. No, it's impossible for her to understand. She had never left Hong Kong, not once.

Was she really that angry? Like what I saw earlier today?

I found some paper and a pen, and I started writing.

*

The next day, we were at Grandma's ward again.

'There was a letter I didn't send out from ten years ago.' It was a lie, as I only wrote it last night. But she turned to look at me, intrigued, and there was a familiar softness in her eyes, like the old times. There were sparkles, too, some kind of hope, excitement, and anticipation. *Give me something good*! Her eyes seemed to say.

Dear Grandma,

As always, thanks for your pocket money. I've used it to buy jasmine tea because the local coffee shop sells those now. I drink the tea by the window sill, people-watch, and now I'm writing a letter to you. Sorry, I've chosen to stay in England because the opportunities are here. Sorry if I barely come back to Hong Kong. I hope you believe that my heart is with you and the family, and I'll be there when you need me. Please forgive me, and may you be healthy and happy as you've always been.

Love, Siu-Ping

I hadn't written in my mother tongue for years. The penmanship was a mess, and some sentences didn't even make sense. Had Grandma spotted that? She opened her working palm and asked for the letter. Tears fell down her face, and her skin glowed. Something had shifted – there was a soul in her, the real one, her original spirit.

My mum added, 'See, Siu-Ping hasn't forgotten us.' She wrapped her arms around my shoulders and squeezed. I wondered if my mum felt abandoned by me too, but she never showed.

'Whatever. My muscle is hurting. Get the nurse for me.' Grandma waved and ordered. Her voice was rustling. She was losing her composure. Perhaps it was an epiphany – that there was no need for her to be strong for everyone else anymore. Her children had all grown up, and their children, and theirs.

So we were scurried out of her ward, and the nurse said this would take a while, so we should come back tomorrow.

But there wasn't a tomorrow for Grandma.

It all happened so fast.

The nurse told us that for her last breath, she was holding my letter and placed it on her heart. 'She passed away in peace and happiness, with no regrets.'

I nodded and stared at her thin, long fingers. The nurse gave me her jade bangle.

Once the white sheet covered her whole body and the nurses pushed her away in a hurry, everything became an assembly line. Even death had to be speedy in Hong Kong. Quick hustle at the morgue. Make up for the dead. White face. Red lips. A standardised funeral. Cremation. Fire. The monk chanted the sacred scripture. Incense. Friends bowed. Family kneeled. My condolences. Thank you, thank you. A little box in the crematory was her final resting place. We kneeled again. Boom boom boom.

I went into Grandma's bedroom that night. After Grandpa died and before she moved to the care home, she'd had my old room so my mum could take better care of her. The air still smelt old, maybe from her winter coats and those incense boxes. My childhood things were mixed with her belongings. By her/my bed, there was also a mooncake box, like mine, beaten too. I opened it, and all my letters were inside, standing up in chronological order. I looked for my first note. It was a hand-drawn card copying the illustration on the mooncake box. I'd added two stick people holding hands under the big yellow moon, one smaller than the other. I'd written with a childish hand:

Dear Grandma,

I like watching the moon with you. Write to me more. You are the Grandma I adore.

Siu-Ping

Fiction

TOFU
Carmen Hoang

At university you told your friend that you couldn't imagine your life without meat. At that point, you'd never had a meal without an animal being involved. You sailed through the courses at Chinese weddings, greedily lapping up dishes of fish, pigs, and lobsters. You and your friends would try to prolong the day together by buying chicken and chips, lounge on the park wall, hands slick with chicken grease and burger sauce. On your way to school your brother bought you a sausage roll from a now long-gone bakery on Edward Street, and for some reason that memory has always meant something to you.

Becoming a vegetarian was one of the hardest things you've ever done. Not because you missed eating animals, but because it meant a door closing on your culture and your traditions. But as the old saying goes, some doors close so others can open. You found strength in principles, learnt to accept mistakes and did your own take on your culture. You discovered new foods and became more adventurous with your tastes.

Chinese and Vietnamese food culture as a vegetarian is a paradox. Both cultures are bursting with delicious vegan and vegetarian dishes but often families will find the idea of cooking a vegetarian meal completely alien. But there's one thing that reaches over the chasm. A vegetarian staple that's existed in East and South East Asian culture for thousands of years. And that's tofu.

SILKEN

As a teenager you sit on the top deck of the 47 bus heading towards Surrey Quays. On the brick walls of Pepys Estate you see the spray painted words: 'REGENERATION IS SOCIAL CLEANSING'. It's the first time you ever think about Deptford as a home, and not just a place. The first time you think about when regeneration becomes gentrification, and who 'regeneration' is for. You watch as buildings and stairways you ran along as a child get torn down, crumbling as easily as silken tofu.

Cut to the present. You open a council letter on how important social housing is to the borough. As they list buildings they're proud of, people on Crossfields Estate are being turfed out of the homes

TOFU

they've lived in for years. You realise that developers use the words 'affordable housing' in place of 'social housing' and hope people don't notice. It takes you a long time to understand that the two are not the same and that words are deceptive.

You're constantly worried that your mum's block of flats is next and you wouldn't know where to begin. The Chinese/Vietnamese community has always been seen as quiet. But recently you've watched it go from delicate to something altogether more powerful, louder. The internet offers arms and helping hands. You just need to reach out and ask.

SOFT

Unlike you, your brothers hated tofu. They complained that it had no flavour but you always loved the way tofu tastes. Your favourite food growing up was minced pork and soy sauce on top of tofu. Protein on protein because your parents couldn't imagine serving a solely tofu dish. You used to mash the tofu up into your rice. You got the feeling your mum thought that was delightfully weird. You make that dish now with soy mince. You still love that mushy texture because it reminds you of being a kid.

Much like a lot of women you know, you've always had a tough relationship with your body. Your community values girls and women who are thin. They are not kind to soft bellies. You used to parrot your mum's anti-fat philosophy in flippant ways, internalising it like a parasite. You don't know when you stopped but at some point you started standing up for yourself and others in her firing line. You worry, though, that it's too late and the damage is done.

As you watch social media and the stream of feeds enveloping everyone around you, you wish your nieces never have to go through what you and your friends did. But at least then when the school bell rung out you got to go home and switch off from playground gossip and insecurities. You think it's going to be so much worse for them than it ever was for you.

FIRM

It's 2016. Your choice to become a vegetarian was largely based on environmental justice. Climate anxiety and optimism smashes in your psyche at age twenty-three. You start hanging around with activists and discover veganism. You watch *Cowspiracy* and realise you pretty much ate a whole cow while backpacking in South America. You think about how indulgent meat production is and how bad it is for the environment. You take things slow: first limiting your meat intake, then becoming a pescetarian because you can't imagine not eating fish. Then your friend's boyfriend tells you fish production is terrible for the environment, too. You reluctantly cut fish out altogether, which is hard because you love those seafood packs from Sainsbury's. Thanks a lot, Friend's Boyfriend.

Your parents do not understand this change. Your dad thinks it's because you love animals. Your mum tells your aunties it's because you're watching your weight. You laugh at the idea of vegetarianism being a diet because your bread consumption has shot up since. Each time you reject your mum's pho she rolls her eyes at you, even though it's been six years. The saving grace is your dad's cooking. You rarely see eye to eye because you're both stubborn and lowkey resentful, but he's always had your back when it comes to your food choices. His tomato and tofu stew is comfort in simplicity.

Family gatherings are . . . tough. You realise how vegetarian unfriendly Chinese wedding banquets are. Your aunt is worried about you because you haven't eaten anything. You tell her you don't eat meat. She tries to get you to eat a bit of lobster because *that's not meat*. You end up eating a bowl of veggie noodles out of a strong twelve-course. You wonder whether this is all worth it.

TOFU

You now have (mock) beef in the Chinese restaurant under the Holiday Inn. You realise how much meat rules not just the Chinese community but Britain as a whole. You read about how the rise in intensive farming in the past five years has led to a damage in biodiversity and a reduction in forests; all to supply us with cheap meat.

EXTRA FIRM

The usual racist, sexist comments you get from strangers takes a nasty turn when the pandemic hits. All the lechy passes, and using your race as a weapon, the *go back to where you came from* and the *didn't realise you spoke English*, everything becomes tinged with something more dangerous. You hear about people who look like you getting attacked, family members spat on and degraded, until your own encounter leaves you crying on the pavement alone. You're so embarrassed and angry at yourself that you never speak about it.

You stay inside and process the world. You gain weight and learn to hate yourself in old ways. But your friends and loved ones pick you up, show you kindness which turns you – not resilient because you've come to dislike that word – but accepting of yourself, each day at a time.

You've recently made one of the worst decisions of your life: you join TikTok. You like it for cooking tips and sketch comedies. You spend a whole night watching an array of tofu dishes being made and can't really fathom how big the tofu market is now. You really love this one video of a Chinese woman making tofu from scratch and are amazed by this two thousand year old process. You think about making your own tofu but that quickly passes when you realise how lazy you are.

You worry that TikTok will swallow you up if you let it because you enjoy the commentary and the positivity. You're so intrigued by what the next generation are doing. They're so funny, they're so principled, they stand firm in a world that is burning against them. In 2019 you went to the Climate March. You were overwhelmed by the kids there, their spirit and their defiance. You think about your nieces and what they'll inherit from us. Because you don't want the world to burn before they get a chance to form their own beliefs and fight their own fights. And as you change your own habits, you hope the world is kind enough to them, and to us all, before it's too late.

WILD WOMEN AND THEIR FRUITS
Kari Pindoria

My mother told me that I was born on the same day as a storm. Like a cannonball, I shot out of her belly and cried in time to the rhythm of the raindrops tapping against the window. She told me that it was the happiest day of her life because my father arrived at the hospital with a box of soggy strawberry shortcakes from her favourite bakery. Until last year, my mother would grab her umbrella and make trips to the small bakery whenever the clouds came out. We would eat the slices in silence on the cold, wooden flooring of the living room, and every now and then, I would see the corners of my mother's mouth slowly turn into a smile. She would always buy an extra cake slice for herself, leaving it perfectly wrapped up in the thin yellow crepe paper, ready for her to tear into the following evening.

    I barely knew my father and felt strangely

indifferent when he left us for another family. Before I moved out for college, I grew up with just my mother in a two-bedroom apartment near the suburbs. She lived her life backwards, sleeping in all day and awake most nights. You could tell when she hadn't got enough sleep because her eye sockets would sink into her ashen face like two craters of a moon. On the mornings when I had to wake up extra early for school, I would slump into the living room, rubbing the sleep from my eyes, to find my mother sewing pieces of fabric together in the armchair against a dimly lit lamp, her back hunched into an arc. She mostly worked night shifts for a ladies' fashion company stacking shelves and tailoring dresses, but she still made sure to never let me go to school or to bed with an empty stomach. I liked the mornings because I knew Ma would leave a plate of apricot danishes, peeled green apples and plums out on the kitchen counter; the apples neatly cut into crescent moon shapes with the seeds carefully plucked out of the core, as if she had used a pair of tweezers. By the time I had got dressed, the kettle would have already been boiled for me; the smoky, rich smell of coffee enveloping the kitchen like a heavy cloak.

Ma cooked the best meals when she was asleep. Even though the meals were simple, only containing a few different ingredients, they were flavourful and just right. The first time I caught her sleep-cooking was in early spring, I think, when the daffodils were beginning to perk up from the ground and the air had that grassy, musky smell. If I was walking home from school with Mina, who preferred to take the scenic route through the fields, I probably had moss sticking to the soles of my sneakers when I stepped into the flat. I was welcomed home by the sounds of a metal cleaver tapping against a chopping board and the humming of water gently bubbling from our rice cooker. I swapped my muddy sneakers for my mule slippers and walked into the kitchen, the fragrance of cooked ginger and garlic getting closer to me with each step.

My mother was sitting on the stool by the counter, chopping a head of white sweetheart cabbage and spring onions whilst still in her silk pyjama suit, her black long hair tied up in a tight bun and her eyes closed. The cupboard doors were all left wide open; the stacks of pots, pans, tinned foods and cereal boxes of different colours on display, sitting patiently the way they might in a supermarket aisle. I thought about the old saying, the one that says you shouldn't wake a sleepwalker suddenly in case they have a heart attack from the shock. She looked peaceful, as if it was the most natural thing in the world, so I decided to sit back and watch her as she gently separated the green long strips of the spring onion from the white bulb. After she was done slicing the scallion, with the same precision she would exert when awake, she stumbled towards the large wok we keep by the hob and began frying the vegetables in oil and soy sauce on medium heat until they caramelised; the delicate white edges of the cabbage turning sticky and dark. I took out a serving spoon from the kitchen drawer and scooped some rice into two deep ceramic bowls; the clumps of rice looked like small clouds and smelled sweet like freshly popped corn. When Ma was done frying the vegetables, she spooned the mixture on top of each rice cloud, and dashed more soy sauce over the top. Then, she finally adorned the dishes with the green spring onion. Still asleep, she used her hands to shovel the rice into her mouth, some of it splattering on her chin and down her clothes, tiny brown dots of soy sauce leaking into the silk.

Mina was at our place when all of the cats from the neighbourhood came to try my mother's watermelon and cucumber juice. It was a warm, late summer afternoon. The sky had streaks and pockets of pink clouds that looked like candy floss, and I could hear the sound of children laughing and playing football in the distance. Even though our living room is smaller than the rest of the rooms in the apartment, I loved seeing the seasons come and go through the tall, glass windows. I admired how the sky cast the living room in a purplish-pink tint; the heat from the sun melting the ice cubes in our glasses of water, the condensation causing little droplets to run down the side of the glass. Mina, who didn't cope too well with the heat, was sprawled on the living room sofa with a cold, wet flannel laid flat on top of her forehead, her legs hanging off the side. I was lying on my front, the tips of my elbows against the floor for balance whilst I dangled my legs up and down in the air. We were both in linen shorts and tank tops, listening to the gentle hum of the electric fan whilst we took it in turns to flip through the glossy art and literature magazines that Ma paid monthly subscriptions for. There was one serial, called Sage, that we were particularly excited to read every month. It was a comic which followed the magical adventures of a half-plant woman who grew out of a seed instead of an egg and got her nutrients through photosynthesis rather than food. I was mesmerised by the artist's illustrations; the fluid, warped drawings filled with vivid colours reminded me of rainbows you see refracted on the top of oil slicks. Sometimes, there would be double-page spreads of wild, spindly foliage merging with the sky and the ground. I closed my eyes, tilting my head closer to the pool of sunlight that beamed on the floor, pretending to be her.

I awoke to the whirring mechanical sound of a blender on high speed. My eyes slowly scanned the room, adjusting to the twilight that was now filtering through the half-drawn blinds. A dark purple glow, a lonely ice cube barely staying afloat in a glass, a crow calling. Mina was no longer on the sofa and left no traces of herself behind. The stacks of magazines we ogled at were neatly slotted back into their designated space on the bookshelf, the wet flannel nowhere to be found, the electric fan tucked away in the corner. I doubted whether Mina had even come over at all, until I heard her laugh echoing from the hallway. She beckoned me to the kitchen. I dragged my feet.

Our apartment was on the ground floor, with our kitchen patio opening up to the communal garden – we shared it with the other residents on the block – through a lovely set of antique French doors. The garden was fairly large, about the size of a college basketball court, and was used a lot more often when I was much younger. Maybe it was because I was only five or six years of age, and had no real concept of time, but it felt as if our neighbours would host gatherings in the garden almost every weekend, inviting their friends from other towns over to sunbathe on rattan chairs, gossip, and eat burgers and skewers that were grilled on a disposable barbecue. A few of the residents were green thumbs so the garden was relatively well maintained; the grass cut, the weeds in between the cracks of the paving stones removed, the hedges trimmed. Mrs. Shaw, the elderly woman who lived a few doors down from us, taught me how to identify different flowers when I was a hyperactive young child. I remember walking up and down the garden with her – she walked with a diamond embellished wooden stick and in brown Birkenstock sandals paired with socks – shouting out the names of the plants we strolled past: yellow-pearled begonias, red-trimmed pansies, and great pink peonies that looked like shower loofahs. But as rent prices went up, a lot of the families we knew from the block moved away, later replaced by younger adults who threw sophisticated dinner parties, with hors d'oeuvres and tall candles in empty wine bottles; or busy commuters who wanted to live affordably but still keep their corporate jobs in sky-rise buildings. The garden was taken care of less and less, and eventually became hard to tame like straggly, unwashed hair. We didn't use the garden much anymore, preferring to sit in public parks instead, so I was surprised to see that the patio doors were on the latch, the white lace curtain tied up in a knot to the side.

Both Mina and Ma were outside, Ma standing barefoot on the tall grass, Mina crouching down wearing a pair of my neon blue Adidas sliders. Ma stood facing the rest of the garden, with her back toward me, her head slightly tilted to the side and her arms hanging down by either side of her, hands limp like wilted flowers. They were both surrounded by a circle of cats lapping from rectangular plastic tupperware containers, which were filled to the brim with a saturated red liquid and placed across the garden in a ring shape, each container set a couple of metres apart from the last one. There were about eight cats in total outside. I watched them for a few moments from inside the kitchen, noticing their differences.

One of the cats was very slender, with a long, pointed tail and short black fur all over its body, except from under the neck where a small tuft of white fur popped out. When he stood up straight it almost looked as if he was wearing a tuxedo, like a doorman standing outside of a fancy hotel. There were three tabby cats, one ginger and the other two a blend of matted brown and grey. They were the most playful of the group and sat the closest to Mina, stretching out their paws to get her attention. Mina gave the tabby cats intermittent neck rubs and belly scratches but kept her distance from them when they tugged the drawstrings of her linen shorts with their claws. A couple of white cats, with unusually long whiskers and bushy tails, were finishing off their last sips of the juice and began slowly walking away from the circle and towards the space under the lime-green acer tree at the back of the garden. I assumed these two were related in some way because their movements were so synchronised, from the way they both retreated to the shade, to the way they groomed themselves and each other. After they had thoroughly licked each other on top of the head, under the neck and near the pinks of their noses, they fell asleep with their bodies entangled in a yin and yang shape.

And then there was one plush grey cat, who sat in a loaf right by Ma's feet, with ears that were folded down like pieces of origami paper. Mina turned her head back as I made my way towards them, excitedly patting her hand on the grass next to her to signal where I should sit. As I walked closer, I peered into one of the containers and saw short strands and clumpy chunks of watermelon flesh bobbing along the top of the liquid like dead fish in a tank.

'She made juice whilst you were both sleeping,' Mina said softly, as she stroked the inside of one of the tabby cat's paws, delicately grazing her finger along its pink pad.

I glanced at Ma. She was slowly lifting her hand up now, gracefully pointing her index finger to the back of the garden where the short wooden fence met the pale sky. Although her eyes were closed, I saw her eyelids fluttering in little tremors like butterfly wings in the wind. At first, we didn't know what she was pointing at but then we heard scratching noises, like the way mice gnaw and skittle inside of rotted walls, the sound so clear and loud, I thought it was coming from the ground beneath us. And then we saw it. A long line of cats jumping onto the fence one by one, balancing briefly there for a moment before galloping their way towards us and into the circle. Whilst the first group of cats looked fairly clean and well groomed, the second group that followed looked dishevelled and forlorn in comparison – their fur unkempt, their claws much longer, their ears tipped at the top. Hungry and scared, they devoured the watermelon and cucumber juice as we sat listening to their sandpaper tongues hitting the liquid, the noise like a clock ticking. Then the sound of gentle purring and the feeling of peace.

Non-fiction

MARIA AND THE RISING SEA
Anne Elicaño-Shields

Maria Francisco, 88, is listening to her favourite noontime *teleserye*. She looks vacantly at a screen, where the sobs of star-crossed lovers are interspersed with a bastardised Taylor Swift song. I want to be helpful so I ask if I should turn up the volume.

'I can hear just fine,' Maria tells me, irritation creeping into her lyrical Ilonggo drawl. 'My ears work so well I can even hear the sea over there.'

She points to a mirror hanging on the wall. It's the size of a dinner serving tray and has seashells strung on nylon fishing thread and pasted in dense rows along the frame. The mirror is a common handicraft from Panay in the Philippines, given as presents or sold for export. It's made by fisher wives from the seaside town in Capiz, which is located in the northeast portion of the island. Maria's mother and grandmother were fisher wives. If Maria had gotten married, the shell mirror would probably have been gifted to a mother-in-law. Instead, when Maria joined my grandmother's household as a maid, age fifteen, the mirror came along with her. It was a thank you present from Maria's mother, for taking her girl from their seaside hut into the bustling capital city of Manila, 398.17 kilometres away. Maria, along with the seashell mirror, stayed with our family for four decades.

My mother and her five siblings called Maria *'yaya'* (nanny). When my mother had children of her own, Maria became my yaya as well. She taught me the names of all the shells that lined the mirror. As a child, I thumbed through each, like my treasured marbles, and parroted back: *knobby starfish, sea snail, turban snail, clam shell, nassa shell and spider conch*.

As a young child, I latched onto Maria's stories of her early life in her seaside home. My small stomach rumbled when she told me that one could make a salad straight off the beach, with sea grapes, uni scooped out of spiky urchin shell, and a drizzle of cane vinegar wine.

She told me about weekend family outings by the seaside, where they brought her elderly grandmother to the beach every Sunday, straight after Catholic Mass. Along with a host of other illnesses, the old woman had weak lungs. The family could no longer afford the costly medicine and hoped that the salt in the sea air would thin the mucus in her system.

I thirsted for pirate stories but there were none. Instead, Maria told me about her older brother, a fisherman who became stone-deaf from blast fishing. This is how it works: the dynamite is hurled away from fishermen's *bangka*, the corals shatter, and then hundreds of fish surface, belly up. Maria's brother botched the throw and swam away with blood in his eyes and a tear in his ear membrane.

Whenever I see the mirror from Capiz, I remember Maria's stories. The mirror now has missing shells and, like a mouth with gapped teeth, doesn't speak. But I know what Maria means about 'hearing' the sea. If you press a shell against your ear it's as if its cold lips are mimicking underwater swells. It's a gentle whisper, unlike the violent gales that Maria heard on November 8, 2013.

Maria had retired and gone back to live with relatives on a leased farm in Capiz. On that fateful morning, Maria woke up to the sound of corrugated metal ripping. Typhoon Haiyan, one of the most powerful tropical cyclones ever recorded, blew away the roof of Maria's shanty. As a result, Maria, along with her neighbours, fled to an evacuation centre.

I ask Maria if she had any idea that the super typhoon was coming. Maria is illiterate but she was attuned to the natural world. Her little plot of land heaved with root crop harvest and rows of orchids propagated from the jungle. Did she see any changes in the wind or the way the clouds looked?

Maria looks at me with weary eyes and reminds me that Capiz had always been Storm Country, with category three typhoons regularly sweeping through. Two days before Haiyan made landfall, *barangay* officials had gone around, sound systems strapped to motorcycles, ordering everyone to evacuate. Maria thought it was just a standard warning. She, along with thousands on the island, didn't know how a super typhoon could ravage their island.

Thousands of miles away from the frontlines of the climate crisis, the Los Angeles Times warned that Haiyan would make Hurricane Katrina, which devastated Louisiana in 2005, 'look like a weak cousin'.

Maria tells me that radio news presenters had used a curious English word as they spoke in their local Ilonggo: 'storm surge'. Even most native English speakers don't know that a storm surge is an abnormal rise of coastal water generated by a storm.

Maria's friends in neighbouring coastal villages spoke of waves rising to seventeen feet high, and how they had to cling to fallen power lines so they wouldn't be swept to sea. Others drowned within minutes. An ocean freighter and floating cars were swept inland, slamming into houses and crushing those caught in the flood.

This isn't the ocean I know from Maria's bedtime stories. This sea did not heal with its salty air, feed with netfuls of fish, or delight with lovely shells. Instead, it birthed a super typhoon that displaced millions and killed thousands. It's what turned Maria, both the narrator and hero of the tales that made children dream, into a climate refugee.

Maria asks me: 'How did this happen? Are we being punished for our sins?'

She believes that the changes in the weather are part of God's will. But even Maria, a devout Catholic, can't wrap her head around this super typhoon of biblical proportions. I try to explain the best way I can. Air pollutants, trapped in the atmosphere, are making the Earth warmer. This global heating has caused ice caps to melt, leading to rising sea levels and temperatures. Higher sea temperatures create stronger cyclones. Sea level rises cause larger storm surges and archipelagos like the Philippines, where many people live near the coast, are particularly vulnerable.

The science is basic and heartbreaking. I tuck it into a pocket in my mind so I can explain it the same way to my young children. They deserve to know –

this is the world they're inheriting from Maria and me.

Maria hasn't met my young children. I'm in Manila for a visit but they've stayed behind with my British husband. We live in Great Britain, an island which – for now – isn't on the frontlines of the climate crisis. But it will come. Already, my children have endured a summer in London where the heat rose to 40°C. Three degrees higher may deform body proteins and damage the brain. When I was my son's age, the hottest day of summer in equatorial Manila was 37°C, and Maria watched as I tried to fry an egg on my grandmother's driveway. If London's hottest summer was three degrees warmer, we would have all turned into human omelettes.

Maria wants to meet my children. I promise I'd take them during the UK school holidays but she sternly shakes her head. 'July through October is typhoon season in the Philippines,' Maria reminds me. I think about Haiyan and all the super typhoons yet to come and wonder if I was wrong to bring children into a world with an uncertain future. Ezra Klein, in The New York Times, says: 'The green future has to be a welcoming one, even a thrilling one. If people cannot see themselves in it, they will fight to stop it. If the cost of caring about climate is to forgo having a family, that cost will be too high. A climate movement that embraces sacrifice as its answer or even as its temperament might do more harm than good.' Is having children bad for the planet? It's abominable to place the burden of the climate crisis on parents when most of the world's pollution is caused by private corporations. Cutting carbon pollution in half by 2030 is what will stabilise the climate and not having kids isn't what will tip the balance . . . policies that step away from fossil fuels and reduce consumption will. My promise to Maria and other climate refugees is this: I will prepare my children for the future. I will raise them to make eco-conscious choices, teach them to grow their own food, and encourage them to be part of climate-resilient communities.

When Maria lost her home to Haiyan, my mother quickly took her back to my grandmother's house in Manila, where she now lives. She's safe, cared for, and loved. But Maria will always be a climate refugee. I'm told by my many aunts that Maria asks the same question every day: 'How is Capiz?'

She asks me the same question now. I tell her how the international community has come together to help our country rebuild houses, schools, health centres. I talk about how floating and sea-floor artificial reefs have been installed, how communities have planted thousands of mangroves that will become a breeding ground for fish. I tell her that, far away from our shores, world leaders at the 2022 UN climate change conference (COP27) agreed to create a global fund to give financial help to developing countries devastated by climate disasters. The climate fund deal is imperfect and only a few governments have significantly pledged money for it. Oil-producing countries and the biggest carbon polluters have watered down attempts to curb the phasing down of fossil fuels. I wonder how this story will end.

I fight the childish instinct to crawl into my former yaya's arms and whimper: *I want our old sea back, not this poisoned ocean that births monstrous cyclones.* Instead, I bite the words down because I don't want to disturb Maria's peace. Climate injustice has already taken so much away from her.

Maria quietly turns and puts her leathery hand over mine. She's always been wise and nurturing but, at this very moment, it's as if she's turned as ancient as Mother Earth.

'Close the window before you leave,' she says. 'A storm is coming.'

Outside, it begins to rain.

Fiction

FRUITING
Lola Pereira

In the warm April sunlight of the dry season, Ama watched the gentle sway of the ube tree's bright purple pears twirl around its avocado-green leaves. She liked to sit under the tree and watch its broad branches bow to her, bringing the fruit closer before pulling away. She imagined she could reach a pear right from where she sat on the ground. The tree shade kept her cool, as long as she stayed beneath its fruit. In their quiet but not quite rural part of the city, her family's backyard was deep, wide and green with grass, fertile enough to grow the wild lawn that her father cut back often and the singular ube tree that sat at the back, forty metres from the house. The longest of the tree's arms dangled fruit teasingly into their neighbours' paved gardens.

Ama. Someone called her from the house. She spun over the cool grass onto her front, her movement startling the tweeting birds. She saw the silhouette of her mother crouched in the shade of the doorway, her mother's apron pulled to one side over bent knees, a bounty of sunlight illuminating the backyard grass between them.

Bring some ube inside, your father wants to cook.

With an improvised basket made from her summer dress, Ama presented her mother with the fruit. Her mother was waiting at the kitchen table, her father already at the stove, his fingers flicking at pots that Ama couldn't quite see but could already smell. The plantain sizzled as he turned over each semi-volcanic slice with bare but hardened fingers and licked at them noisily after each flip to taste and cool.

Her mother rolled the pears from one hand to another, feeling for the ripe ones, her mouth twisting either disappointingly or remaining neutral. She placed the best ones in a bowl next to the stove. The rest rolled around on the kitchen table. In the shade of the doorway, Ama stood and watched the ube tree's pears glisten like coloured raindrops.

She hoped that moving away from the most beautiful tree she had ever known would be worth it, that moving for *work and opportunity* as her parents had called it, would be worth the sacrifice.

She had tried to reason with her parents. She remembered that Uncle Bola and his wife had gone to London for *work and opportunity* and soon returned home. *Work and opportunity* had brought the loudest argument Ama had ever heard. The backyard that they returned to was replete with dried soil and fallen trees, almost as if the trees wanted to show them what it meant to be abandoned, to leave beauty for money. She argued that their neighbours, Uncle Bola's neighbours, had left and returned too, and although their backyard remained intact, their marriage had not and the children, according to their Sunday school rumours, lived with alternating parents weekly.

Our *work and opportunity* will be greater, Ama's father's eyes whispered between gulps over the kitchen table. His head barely up from his ube and roasted corn, his wife nodding into her own bowl, licking at the stew on her fingertips. It felt like a lot of *work* to be moving and their *opportunity* was sitting in their backyard providing them all with the sweetest summer shade. Ama picked the roasted skin of the ube and gnawed hungrily at the bright green flesh, savouring the taste as she ripped the fibres away from the large stone.

Ama slept most of the way on the airplane away from her old house. The sprawling reach of the ube tree danced across her eyelids as she dreamed. She slept most of the way to the new flat, her eyes briefly opening to see flashes of her green garden dissipate in her memory, taken over by this England's – this London's – series after series of concrete buildings, the taxi's pine cone air freshener a reminder of a false promise.

Ama was carried all of the way up in the building's lift, tucked into the familiar sweat of her father through his brown wool jacket. It helped to mask the week-old urine residue in the corner of the lift. She was laid on the living room sofa to rest more until sleep slowly loosened its hold on her. Ama awoke and looked around. The stucco effect that had coated the outside of her house in Lagos in its brown paint was now replicated on the inside in white over the ceiling and the walls.

The flat was furnished – and nothing felt familiar. None of this was hers. With the balcony door open, car horns and tyres screeching climbed up the tower block walls to reach Ama's ears. She followed the sound to the balcony, tucked her red jacket around herself and slipped into her jellied sandals.

Ama didn't know how far up she was but she could see tightly-packed houses for miles across London. With only a few spots of green spaces where the grass was presumably cut low, the trees rose almost randomly and their leaves swayed in the blustery wind.

The wind at Ama's height whipped furiously around her, a raw welcome embracing her sandaled toes. The wind carried cold water droplets from the city's grey clouds and the rain coated Ama's arm across the edge of the balcony. She shivered.

A window tapped behind her. A neighbour's hand scratched at the lace behind their curtain. A face smiled and waved, then disappeared. Ama's mother appeared behind her, a hand on one shoulder, her face tucked in next to Ama's on the other side. She pointed at a corner of the empty and unswept balcony. Ama's eyes caught the cobweb holding onto dead, paper thin leaves. She hoped she could crush them underfoot before they were removed. She loved that feeling.

In that space there, her mother starts, we'll be able to plant some vegetables and herbs. We won't have the ube but we can find something just as good and tasty for us to grow here or something just as tasty in the market.

Ama nodded.

Do you know what you'd like to grow?

Ama shook her head. There was nothing more beautiful than the ube tree they had in their backyard. Ama's mother raised her index finger out of the balcony and into the distance.

Your new school is just down there.

Ama lifted herself onto tiptoes and peered over the edge a little more. Rain tip-tapped at her face. She felt her mother's arm on her shoulder move down to her waist and pull her closer. Her school building looked like window frames on all the sides she could see.

It's called Deptford Park Primary, Ama. There are monkey bars in the playground, basketball hoops and hopscotch.

That's stupid, Ama thought. She couldn't see any of that. She only saw the grey concrete painted darker by the rain.

Ama! Her father called from back inside the flat. He was hovering by the living room door. Change your shoes. We'll bring back some food.

He handed her a new pair of black trainers and waited for her to put them on as he swung keys around his index finger. Ama danced her fingers around the soft black laces, swirled them around the shiny silver-looking eyelets until her fingers met the black leather and bubbled soles. Standing in the lift with her father, when the light stopped flickering with the temperamental power of flying insects, Ama gasped at the purple and white lights emitting their own silent siren from the bottom of her trainers. With lights as deep purple as her favourite fruit, she danced and politely stomped her way through their shopping expedition, despite the rain.

It was still raining on Ama's first day of school. Ama was introduced to the class and was given an empty seat close to the window looking out on the concrete playground. She thought of her final day with her ube tree. Ama had rolled around in its cool shade and dipped out of it only to drink water and eat with her parents. The bright purple of the fruit's skin and its savoury and squishy lime green insides were tangible though now faraway memories. In the playground at breaktime, she splashed in puddles under the school's largest fruitless tree.

The weather cleared up in June for Ama. She noticed the incessant spring rain had stopped in England. The high street was awash with bright clipped male voices as soon as the weekend's light hit pavements and the street sellers' melodic cadences reached her bedroom window. She remembered the freedom of being outside in the warmth and under the sun or shade as soon as the day renewed itself.

She placed her class day trip permission slip on the partially folded dining table and ran back to her bedroom window to listen to the community waking up.

Ama's mother waved her and her classmates off on the coach from their school. Ama was pleased to sit next to Cherry on the coach. Cherry smelled like artificial cherry lip balm and offered it to everyone, carefully unwrapping a new stick each week that she said her big sister *earned* from Superdrug. Ama loved pointing out the trees and their species along the way to someone who would listen and not make fun of her for talking about her beloved ube tree. But Ama didn't think she would say she was making friends just yet.

Ama was astounded at the number of trees and the greenery she saw at Kew Gardens. The grasses and flowers, leading to other grand trees, were like heaven. She wanted to go everywhere. The teachers and chaperones encouraged them to walk around the enclosure but not stray too far from the Temperate House – the biggest glasshouse Ama had ever seen – and not to touch anything. Twirling the stick of cherry lip balm up and down in its case, Cherry used the stick as a makeshift compass to lead her and Ama around the outside of the Temperate House until Ama noticed they had done two loops of it. She stopped them at a door.

Can we go in here?

Cherry paused to twist the lip balm low into its case, running it over her lips twice before pocketing it. Ama opened the iron door and jumped a little when it slammed shut behind them. The Temperate House was warm. It tasted like the wet season for Ama, the glass roof keeping all the warmth and moisture in. Ama felt tiny droplets of water form on her face. Cherry smacked her lips, her lip balm melting into a sticky gloop. She wiped her lips with the back of her hand, then wiped her hand on her summer dress. They looked around and up to the top of the Temperate House – it was filled with bright and swooping plants dotted around at different levels and wrapped around a central staircase. There were all sorts of trees settled next to each other, different tropical species wrapped around each other, and richly green plants spiralling around the House – all with their names stuck on placards in front of them.

Ama called Cherry to follow. The girls dipped under drooping branches and posed for fake photographs with wild plants. Cherry stopped at the raised edge of a large tree to rest under the shade and pulled Ama down to sit beside her. From their corner of the glasshouse, they watched their classmates run round in circles, skidding and slowing down over the mossy paving stones, leaning in to smell the brightest plants.

Ama closed her eyes and rolled her head back. Being surrounded by so much greenery, made her miss the tree she had grown up with even more: her ube tree. Ama was reminded of days spent laying beneath the tree, reaching her hands up to grasp as much of the ube as she could, as the branches bowed down to her. When they rose to breathe, she rose to reach them, and wiggled her fingers until her fingertips cradled the ube in the soft palm of her hand.

You're not allowed to touch it, Ama.

Ama blinked and felt an arm pull at her wrist. In her right hand, she held an ube fruit loose and soft; moisture from the Temperate House, from the tree, trickling down her fingers and onto the back of her right hand. Stuck between awe and fear, she lowered the fruit to her lap and felt Cherry's eyes on her.

Is that the purple fruit that you told me about?

Ama nodded. She held the ube and looked back up at the tree. She couldn't resist. Ama pulled Cherry's lip balm from her hand and used the sharp rigid base to slice down the middle of the fruit as through butter. Cherry gasped at the bright green insides. Ama held the fruit higher between them as if in offering and beamed at Cherry, already imagining the lime-green fibres between their teeth.

Non-fiction

THE BLUE SHOP
Yuebai Liu

Every Thursday I get bánh mì. No matter what kind of a Thursday it is, I will get up, take a shower, put on fresh clothes, walk to Deptford High Street and get a bag of baguettes filled with pork cuts, pâté, coriander, cucumber and pickled carrots. This isn't a particularly unique bánh mì in today's London food scene; it doesn't contain rare ingredients and the vegetables don't come with a farm-to-table story, the kind that mentions sustainable, seasonal, organic and small-scale all in the same sentence.

It's not from a fancy market stall or a quirky kitchen pop-up, but it is sold twice a week in limited quantities at a small, but mighty Vietnamese grocery store in Deptford. The storefront is blue, a faded yellow sign says *oriental store, open every day, till late*. I call it The Blue Shop.

If my maths is correct, I would say I had at least forty-two bánh mì in 2022. But to be honest, the real number is probably closer to eighty-four, taking into account the times I have had two in a day and the many odd ones I had outside my sacred ritual. *Why the obsession*, I hear you ponder. The truth is I don't fully know, but I suspect it's not just about my bread and meat intake.

Let's start with the shop, home to an abundance of East and South East Asia's food staples that make nostalgic immigrants like myself sigh with relief. Sure, Sainsbury's has a 'World Foods' aisle where I can find soy sauce and Kimchi, but being able to browse and choose from a range of bottled soy sauce, each with a different brewing method and taste profile, brings me joy.

Then there's the bánh mì. Vietnamese for bread and indiscriminately used for any sandwich involving Asianesque fillings in the West. This particular one is the kind you may find at any bánh mì vendor in Hanoi for breakfast or for a snack. Although I'm not Vietnamese and I did not grow up eating the same bánh mì, my Thursday rituals quell, if only a little, my yearning for a past childhood.

Perhaps it's in the name itself, the word for bread in my parents' native Wenzhounese, a vernacular Chinese language that only exists in its spoken form, is pronounced mì bóh with similar intonations. Or it's the anonymity of this specific bánh mì that reminds me of the Wenzhounese snacks my mom would find and buy for me in Rome, where I grew up. After school, I'd often get flat bread with a savoury filling made by a fellow Wenzhounese lady I called Auntie. It couldn't be bought anytime, only twice a week at 5pm at a local Asian grocery store.

Similarly, fresh bánh mì is placed on the cashier counter in The Blue Shop every Thursday around 10am. Wrapped in white baguette paper, they come with a separate resealable bag of pickled shredded carrots that resemble a bag of weed, like those one got off the street in the 2000s, with no labels, no strain names or logos.

They disappear fast as word increasingly gets around and others have the same craving as I do on this day. One time I came in the late afternoon and they were all gone.

'A guy bought them all for his friends. Office lunch!' the owner of The Blue Shop, and who I refer to as Auntie, told me. *They* know, I feared as I remembered the young and cool professionals in the co-working space I walked past earlier. I imagined that these are the only offices where colleagues are friends and will buy Vietnamese baguettes for each other.

I also wondered if the same people would have turned their nose up at the mere sight of unlabelled food in an Asian shop just a few years ago, you know, before smelly foods like fish sauce and kimchi became trendy. Places like The Blue Shop are hidden corners of comfort for the heart-aching diaspora, East and South East Asian immigrants who seek a space to unclench and daydream. Now that *our* food is accepted in popular culture, *they* want a share of that too. I supposed it was better than having our food called gross and it was good for the auntie's business.

Deptford High Street has been branded by the media as one of the coolest streets in the world in 2022, ranking 17th following a Time Out survey. The BBC reported the street as 'varied, culturally rich.' The Mirror echoed the sentiment and reported, 'The area is frequented by cool people,' and so more cool people visit the street, searching for a taste of what varied and culturally rich means.

In truth, this half mile high street *is* ethnically, religiously, linguistically and artistically rich. There is a market that has been selling fresh fish, fruits and vegetables since 1872, there are West African fabric stores, Vietnamese and Chinese restaurants, a Baroque church, a Biltong bar and so on.

Everytime I walk up this half mile street and visit The Blue Shop I discover and learn something about myself. It might be an ingredient, a word, or a piece of history we, the heart-aching diaspora, share. Seasons and events dictate the rhythm of the fruits, spices and snacks sold there. What may at first seem like random cakes and dumplings appearing on shelves and in fridges, I later realise they each mark an imminent special event and a change of season for many East and South East Asians in London.

Bánh ú, for example, is sticky rice with either savoury or sweet fillings wrapped in bamboo leaves and usually eaten on the New Year in Vietnam. Different variations exist in nearby regions, reflecting centuries old migration and trading routes in this part of the world. In each place, migrants adapted, compromised and reinvented their ancestral food to suit their surroundings, using local ingredients and sometimes giving them new meaning.

In Mandarin, it's Zongzi and in Cantonese, it's Joong, usually prepared to celebrate the Dragon Boat Festival in June. In Japan, it's called Chimaki, and it celebrates Children's Day in May. In Myanmar, phet htoke is the same sticky rice triangle stuffed with coconut flesh and sugar steamed in banana leaves for Thingyan, the New Year water festival usually in mid-April. In Singapore, Malaysia and Indonesia it's bak-chang brought by Hokkien immigrants from Fujian, in South East China. In my parents' native Wenzhou, a coastal city just north of Fujian, it's known as Tzon. My mother prepares it each time she visits London, regardless of the time of year. To her, it's special all year round.

Upon entering the shop, I never go straight to the bánh mì, I leave it until the end so I can savour the smells and colours around me. The pungent smell of dehydrated vegetables and shiitake makes my nose twitch. That almost sulphurous smell brings me back to my grandparents' kitchen in Wenzhou, a place I spent many childhood summer breaks and a familiar place I trust, to cook and eat anyway.

The first thing I always see when I go to The Blue Shop is a notice board on the wall populated with handwritten notes and fliers. Today, one advertises a room for rent in Charlton in Vietnamese. Another one gives instructions in English to potential bystanders of immigration raids in Lewisham, along with a support helpline for detainees. Words such as, 'Don't walk by! We can resist the raids together!' and, 'Make sure people know they don't have to answer any questions and can leave' stand out. On the bottom right, in small text it says that the leaflet is produced by SOAS Detainee Support.

There's also a poster shouting about the next Lunar New Year celebrations, an event that usually occurs between January and February, but falls at a slightly different date every year.

On this particular poster, the message is in Vietnamese with the word *Tết*, the term for New Year,

THE BLUE SHOP

highlighted in big bold fonts. The same advertisement is also found down the street, on the store window of a Hokkien grocery store, but in Chinese ideograms.

How isolating it must have felt for the diaspora when The Blue Shop hadn't opened yet. I wonder if there was an equivalent space or notice board in the 80s when Vietnamese refugees who relocated here after decades of experiencing violence, loss and displacement were also silently facing the challenges of having to integrate in a new country. When my parents migrated to Italy from a village in South East China in the 80s, there were no Asian grocery stores, but they kept informed about vital information, usually about accommodation, work and changes in residence permit laws, through Chinese restaurants. Owners and workers at those restaurants were the ears for, and mouth of, the diaspora; they carried all the news and gossip.

Next is a wall of instant noodles from every corner of East and South East Asia. Ah, instant noodles. A staple for newly immigrated Asian working class families, who struggle to find time to cook for their children, exhausted after working impossible hours in order to make a better life, to make ends meet. My immigrant parents were short of time, yes, but they also weren't fully aware of the nutritional value of instant noodles, or rather lack thereof, and I took full advantage. Instead of crisps and burgers, I had instant noodles that came in different shapes, with different seasonings and from different regions: seafood cup noodles from Japan, hot and sour potato noodles from Chongqing, Laksa from Singapore, artificially flavoured Phở Gà from Vietnam and so on.

My parents are no longer struggling, but I stand here silently gazing at the different packages feeling a sense of nostalgia for a distant past. After much deliberation, I decide what seems like the least unhealthy compromise, a few packs of wholewheat baked, rather than fried, noodles. It's still a magical treat.

Along the short, but packed route to the cashier, I recognise variations of ingredients and dishes that accompanied my summers spent at my grandparents, foods I both loved and loathed. Many of these I only knew by their Wenzhounese name, a language that does not have a written script. Seeing them in The Blue Shop, labelled in English and sometimes Vietnamese is like revisiting foods I've known so well in childhood, but now with subtitles.

I now had a language to describe the type of tofu I love. It's an especially firm and brown tofu that's been braised in five spice powder stock, and even in much of East Asia, it's only readily available in specific cities, like in my parents' native Wenzhou.

THE BLUE SHOP

I also learned that when it comes to spices, ingredients and dishes, their nationalities and country borders matter much less than their histories, names and languages. Ironically, there isn't a place where it is more obvious than in The Blue Shop, a generic oriental store where East and South East Asian produce are all lumped together, sharing shelves and refrigerators. Phở rice noodles are not placed on a Vietnamese shelf for example, instead one sees the continuum of different sizes and shapes of rice noodles, each coming from a different and sometimes neighbouring region. The food here has no borders, and I've learned to substitute ingredients and mix spices from different regions. Vietnamese rice noodles drenched in a mix of Korean Gochugaru and Chinese sesame paste, garnished with Japanese pickled mustard greens and bean sprouts, is pretty good.

On every visit, I spend a little more time here. I look for an excuse to stay just a tiny bit longer, to see a new corner I had missed before, or to revisit one I hadn't studied for long enough. The Blue Shop is a corner in Deptford where I can take shelter from the present outside, and find calm in a piece of a faraway place that never existed, not like this. It was never just about the bánh mì.

Fiction

MANGSHO-BHAAT
Santanu Bhattacharya

It takes me a few weeks to figure out what's wrong.

I'm watching a cookery show on TV. It's a weekend and I'm alone in the flat. I made myself a sandwich and brought it to the sofa. The show is an Australian competition, the contestants have boarded a bus to be taken to the outskirts of Melbourne, and then they are entering the home of an Indian-looking lady. It turns out that they are there to cook something called *pasta-not-pasta*, a dish with Indian ingredients devised by this lady. I chomp on my sandwich and watch as the contestants stumble through the process, making the batter of gram-flour and yoghurt, getting it wrong, having to do it again, spreading it over the counter in a thin layer, then cooling it, cutting it into strips, and as someone spreads the batter out too thick, the others exchange glances and shake their heads, *he's going home today*! What comes out in the end is a dish that is not dissimilar in looks to pasta, though it is flavoured with Indian spices and the yellow of the turmeric is too bright for anything Western, the strips seem more slippery and with less of a bite.

Back in the kitchen, I'm clearing out the crumbs and putting away the plate when it strikes me. Khandvi! Of course, that is what they were cooking! And then I realise that not once over the course of the hour-long episode did anyone mention the name. Khandvi, a Gujarati dish that I've eaten before but presented in a different way, the strips stacked in soft rolls one over the other, garnished with coriander leaves and pudina chutney. 'Khandvi,' I say it out loud. Not a difficult word at all, definitely less of a mouthful than *pasta-not-pasta*. Suddenly I'm upset with the Indian lady who hosted the experience. What had stopped her from using the original name? Did she feel that the only way to sell her food was to call it something that white people could not only say, but also relate to? Pasta-not-pasta! Even being purely judged for its creativity, it's a shit name. This draws a laugh from me, and I'm standing in the kitchen chuckling to myself, thinking how we are always simplifying and obliterating our food, our clothes, our festivals, our lives, to make them more palatable for white people. Would a British person living in India ever name their fish-and-chips *maach-aloo-bhaaja*, or an Italian person selling spaghetti have to call it *shimai-not-shimai*? As I'm laughing, I come up with more names for

Western dishes in subcontinental languages, and they all sound so comic that I'm surprised the people who went along with *pasta-not-pasta* didn't just laugh the name away in the first instance.

And that's when I realise what is really wrong here. The sandwich, the one I just made myself with brie and cranberry jam between two slices of rye sourdough. Ever since I moved to this flat, I've mostly been eating sandwiches, experimenting with different kinds of bread, jams, jellies, cheese – cheddar, mozzarella and camembert – things I'd never seen in supermarkets in India, or never paid attention to even if they were there.

After I arrived in London from Mumbai, for the couple of weeks I was staying at a hotel, just before this flatshare got sorted, I'd gone out to Indian restaurants a few times, but the food was mostly subpar and costly, and when I moved here, I decided to eat in as much as possible. Sometimes my flatmates and I have nights in together. Camille, Jake and I will cook pasta, or have fajitas one night a week. In those initial weeks in London, I'd picked up a newspaper outside a Tube station that carried an article about a white British landlord who had refused to rent his house out to an Indian family because, as he put it, *the place would smell of curry wouldn't it*. Perhaps that is what I've secretly feared – that if I made Indian food in this kitchen, the whole flat would smell of spices, and I'm not sure what Jake and Camille would say, whether it would be inconvenient, would they disapprove, regret their decision to make me their flatmate. And so all I've been having is sandwiches, but it's not what I grew up eating, it doesn't always fill me. I wake up hungry in the middle of the night and have to gobble down biscuits. I get headaches in the afternoon sometimes. At least the pasta-not-pasta lady cooks her Indian food, even if she hides its name. I, on the other hand, don't even do that.

My heart warms at the thought of rice and chicken curry right now. Mangsho-bhaat. I don't care that it's past lunch time, that I've just eaten and am not hungry. I pick up my keys and wallet and rush to the shop at the corner of the street, it's called ABC Mini-Mart and sells all kinds of Indian ingredients – spices, herbs, grains, seeds. I've been there before, and I can tell it is run by a Bangladeshi gentleman, because accents don't lie, and whenever we open our mouths to say hello or thank you, our eyes rest on each other for just a while longer, like we're assessing where the other could be from, how new they are to this country, constructing the other person's story in our heads, the familiarity filling in the gaps in facts, the way I can never do for someone not from my part of the world. He can tell the kind of job I work in, that my accent is very South Asian hence I'm a relatively newer arrival, that I've never bought any subcontinental ingredients because I don't cook my food at home. I can tell that he's been in this country for a while, his vowels are rounded, his inflections more British, but the underlying accent is still from the eastern part of the subcontinent. I can tell from how he says some words that he is Bangladeshi, not Indian or Pakistani. Also because some ingredients in his shop have labels in Bangla, and he sells panch-phoron, which I've never seen in the supermarkets. But even though we can deduce so much about each other, we never go beyond the transactional. I don't know his name, nor he mine. I don't know where in Bangladesh he is from, whether he owns this shop or works here, if he lives in the neighbourhood or has to commute from far away. There is something that stops us from going further, leaning into those common origins.

This afternoon, I grab a basket from outside the entrance and walk in with gusto. I'm not here to shop for a meal, I'm here to stock my kitchen up from scratch. The thought of mangsho-bhaat has got my juices flowing, but I won't rush this, I will take my time. This must be an important event in every immigrant's life, setting their kitchen up for the first time, the place that will sustain and fulfil them. We are a generation of vagabonds, swept up in our capitalistic needs of job titles and comforts and assets, moving from city to city, country to country, our ties to our roots shrivelling by the day. Some of us don't speak our languages very well, have forgotten our songs, never read our texts. Our children will know even less, citizens of a homogenous world of which Peppa Pig is Madame Presidente. Maybe then food is the last bastion of our relationship with the past, that no matter how many foreign cuisines we adopt, how many fancy names we learn to say correctly (I still remember when the first Pizza Hut opened in Indian cities, how we learnt to say *peet-zaa*, and laughed at the ones who didn't say it right); in our stomachs, we still crave what our parents and grandparents put on the table at mealtimes.

My hands are moving at lightning speed, dropping anything familiar into the basket – basmati rice, moong dal, toor dal, masoor dal, dhone, jeere, holud, morich, garam masala, panch-phoron, kalo shorshe, kari pata, heeng, salt, sugar, shorsher tel, pickles. I turn into the next aisle to pick up onions, potatoes, tomatoes, ginger, garlic, coriander leaves, tej pata. I nearly bump into an Indian couple who are carefully examining tomatoes for any dents or black spots, out of habit, like they would at the vegetable cart on an Indian street, making sure the seller isn't cheating them, even though there is no need for it here, all products are pre-checked, sanitised and plastic-packaged, only the best quality ones are imported anyway, leaving our people to eat the subpar food injected with pesticides as we send our top produce westward for white people to consume. As usual, the couple size me up, a quick practised look from head to foot, placing me on the map, my job, my income class, my newness, a stolen glance at my brimming-over basket. In return, I size them up as well before busying myself. Finally, I turn into the cold aisle and grab packets of chicken thighs. I take the ones on the bone, because my mother always says that is how it tastes the best, through the juices that are released from the bones and spread into the curry, the meat itself has no taste of its own. She never orders boneless chicken when we go to a restaurant, she doesn't understand how boneless chicken is more expensive than the ones on the bone!

At the till, the Bangladeshi gentleman is trying to play it cool, but is intrigued by what I've bought and how much. This is the first time he's seen me buy these things, and I can't tell if he's impressed or vindicated. When he's entered the full haul into his system, he tells me the amount, which sounds preposterous, but I don't pay attention, I just take my card out and insert it in the machine and enter the PIN, then I nod to him in a thank you.

MANGSHO-BHAAT

'Have a nice day,' he says routinely.

I carry the bags out through the narrow aisle, my arms stretched from the weight.

In the flat, I take a wok out from one of the cupboards. I don't know if it belongs to Camille or to Jake, or was there before they arrived, but I can ask these questions later. I hurriedly cut open all the packets of ingredients, find a large roasting tin and empty the chicken into it, then go about preparing my marinade. At this point, I slow down. I'm not a seasoned cook, I know I will mess this up if I rush. I grab a knife and make diagonal slits on the thighs so the marinade will seep through. I apply a generous layer of salt, turmeric and chilli powder, grind the ginger and garlic into a paste and pour it over, then grate half an onion into the mix, my eyes watering. I try to decide which of the two pickles I should use – lemon-chilli or garlic, but add a little bit of both in the end, what the hell. I spoon copious amounts of yoghurt onto the whole thing, squeeze a full lime, and finally add what my mother says is her magic touch – a dollop of tomato ketchup. Doing this makes me miss her terribly. I decide to take a photo and send it to her when it's done. Then I artfully massage all the embellishments onto the chicken, turning the pieces this way and that, rubbing the mixture on the slits, my hands covered in spices all the way up to my wrists. After I'm done, I lick a bit of the mixture from my fingers, and close my eyes to savour the taste. *Ishhh, it could have bits of raw meat*, I hear my mother's voice in my ears, coming up behind me on those Sunday afternoons when we cooked lunch together, the aromas mixing with those coming from other households, the sounds of vessels clattering, of families chattering, of the TV playing cartoons non-stop to calm the children while fathers snoozed and mothers made rice in pressure cookers, the whistles going off at more and more frequent intervals, and I would lick my fingers again to tease her.

Once I've put the tin in the fridge for the marinade to congeal and slowly make its way into the meat, I begin to slice the onions, making sure they're thin half-moons, the translucent layer coming off at the top. I peel and dice the potatoes, then put them in boiling water to cook. I cut the tomatoes, chop up the coriander leaves, pour vegetable oil into the wok and wait for it to heat up, then add the panch-phoron seeds. When they start to crackle, the smell that wafts up my nostrils is heaven, one of the best cooking fragrances. If we Bengalis were a more enterprising people, like the Italians or the Punjabis, if we could make a big hue and cry about our food, set up restaurants, win Michelin stars, tell tearful stories about our nonnas, panch-phoron would be our gift to the culinary world

MANGSHO-BHAAT

– a combination of five seeds, cumin, brown mustard, fenugreek, fennel, and nigella. But we think of food as something to put on the table, to feed our families and guests, to not charge money for. When people tell us our food is delicious, we smile shyly and invite them home again.

The panch-phoron seeds are crackling, and it's time for the next step. There is an art to knowing this. Often, I've waited too long and the seeds have started to burn, smoke billowing from the oil, the seeds turning charred, shrinking into little black dots. I lower the flame and add the onions, sautéing with a wooden spoon to brown them, add the remaining ginger-garlic paste, cut some green chillis and sprinkle on the oil. I stare at this concoction – there is something satisfying about watching all this beautiful produce coming together harmoniously. Did our ancestors discover each ingredient, cook them over woodfire, decide what to do with them, what brings out the best in each? Was there a council of village elders assembled for every meal, certifying techniques and recipes? What I'm doing now, in this flat very far away from my ancestors' land, is at the end of a long continuous line of collective innovation, and put this way, I'm doubly ashamed that I stopped myself from cooking all these weeks.

When the onions have browned, the tomatoes

cooked, the curry base done, I take the chicken out, the marinade now thick in the middle, slack on the sides, the juices from its various components having released. This is exactly how it should be. I upturn the tin and let the chicken drop into the oil. The wok goes wobbly for a second, then settles down. Smoke rises from it like a soul leaving a body. The whole affair is a noisy one, the oil, the chicken, the base, the juices, all conferring like a reunion of old friends. The smell goes straight to my head, and I have to close my eyes to withstand the shock.

When I open my eyes, I feel a presence behind me without even turning. It's Jake. I'm not sure when he's entered, or how long he's been watching me. I can tell he is taken aback, his jaw slack, lips parted ever so slightly, backpack still on his shoulders, biking helmet in his hand. I smile at him, and he smiles back, unsure.

'What's cooking?' he asks.

'Oh, just some curry,' I play it cool.

'Oh *that* I can tell! My word, you've worked up quite the smell here, haven't you?' *Smell* – one of those English words, could go either way – did he mean *aroma*, or did he mean *stink*? In our languages, *smell* is just one word, no synonyms, but you'd know whether it's a good or bad smell just by looking at the person. They'd close their eyes, inhale, bob their heads and smile – or scrunch up their nose and exhale in short bursts until you'd be in no doubt. Maybe the British need so many words in their dictionary because they've trained their faces to give away nothing. Jake looks around at the smoke in the kitchen. 'Do you mind if I open the windows?' I shake my head, guilty that I should've done it myself. For the last hour that I've been cooking, I've been completely lost to the experience, so I rush to open the window next to me while Jake opens the ones in the living room. He comes back and peers into the wok, squinting his eyes to deconstruct the melange of things, then heads off to his room.

The chicken will take around half an hour to cook. I look around the kitchen, survey the mess, packets strewn all over, bits of colourful powder on the countertop, peels and skins on the floor, spoons and ladles and bowls in the sink. I'm feeling despondent now, what if the spices have stained the counter forever, I haven't even thought about whether there are containers for all these ingredients, haven't checked who these vessels belong to, what if they smell of curry for days, have I taken too many liberties? I kick myself for not having thought this through. I know white people are very particular about the rules of living, how things are used, who shares what, whether the right permissions have been sought. Camille once texted me about whether she could use my pen – *my pen*! I didn't even know it was my pen until she sent a picture to double-check. And here I am, kicking up a storm, stinking things up, leaving indelible marks. I begin to clear up in a huff, making more of a mess, things slipping between my fingers, crash-landing on the floor, spilling over. I've forgotten about the chicken altogether, and I suddenly remember that it needs more water. Panic shoots up my spine. Have I already spoilt the dish, all this brouhaha for nothing?

'Ooh-la-la!' It's Camille in the doorway. She walks up to the hob and lifts the lid, a smile crossing her mouth as she marvels at the boiling curry, hot bubbles popping on the surface. 'It needs water,' she says, and proceeds to add some. 'This much okay?' she asks. 'Some more?' she checks as I shake my head, then she closes the lid and looks around. 'You must be exhausted! How long have you been working on this?' I tell her I've been at it since this afternoon, and it's only now I notice that it's almost dark and nearly dinnertime. 'You need some help,' she says with authority and puts her bag down in a corner, then starts picking up the different packets, making space on the shelves, clearing out old stuff. 'You take care of the sink, I'll put these away.' I thank her, turn away to face the sink, relieved that she's here. As we work, we exchange notes on cooking, whether we like it, how good we are at it, whether we cook often, what kinds of dishes we can make. She asks about the chicken curry, what's special, is this how it's made in India. Of course not, she corrects herself, that can't be, every region would have its own recipe. I tell her about the panch-phoron – that is an eastern thing, and about the marinade that is my own invention, and that it's free and easy really, because every time I add something new to it. I say that the beauty of a curry is that it can take anything, it's not hard and fast, it's one big melting pot. 'I like that idea,' she says, 'One big melting pot.'

Jake now comes out of his room. He goes straight to the hob and lifts the lid. I have to admit that I am liking this, the communal activity that has suddenly come out of my very personal and impromptu act of rushing to the shop. Jake's eyes are like a child's, wide and curious. 'Should I stir it?' he asks before touching the ladle, like the curry is a fragile possession, and I'm its master. 'My mum always grates some nutmeg into a curry. She usually makes it for Thursday dinners,' he says. I ask if we have nutmeg, and that if he wanted he could add some. He and Camille both excitedly set about finding the nutmeg, and when he unearths it, he grates the nut with gusto. Fine powder drops into the curry. 'I'm not sure how much,' he mumbles as he does it, eyes focused diligently on the wok. Then he suddenly stops and turns towards me, his eyes have changed, there's a slight terror in them, the crimson crawling rapidly over his pale skin. 'I'm not, I mean, this is okay right? For me to add something?' Of course, I say, why wouldn't it be? 'Isn't this cultural appropriation?' he asks. 'Like, *you* put in all this effort to make this dish that is a part of *your* culture, and I walk in and grate some fucking nutmeg into it like I know what I'm doing. . .' His voice is despondent, like everything is lost, but I stop him right there, it's completely fine, there's no appropriation here, we're cooking food and it will taste fabulous! Jake nods, unconvinced but relieved.

When the curry is done, I sprinkle garam masala and mustard oil over it, before giving it one last stir. I snap a photo and send it to my mother. Camille has folded, tucked and put everything away, while Jake has set the table. I've also managed to make rice on the side, spiced it with ghee and cumin. Jake and Camille have already taken their seats.

But I need to do just two more things. I turn to my friends. 'So, before we start, in Bangla, this is called mangsho-bhaat.' I don't want to do a *pasta-not-pasta* on my dish.

'Mangsho-bhaat,' they repeat like primary school students.

MANGSHO-BHAAT

'And another thing, it's best eaten with your hands, licking your fingers. I understand if you're not used to eating that way, but that's how I will be eating it.' They say they don't know how to eat that way, but they'd love to try if I showed them.

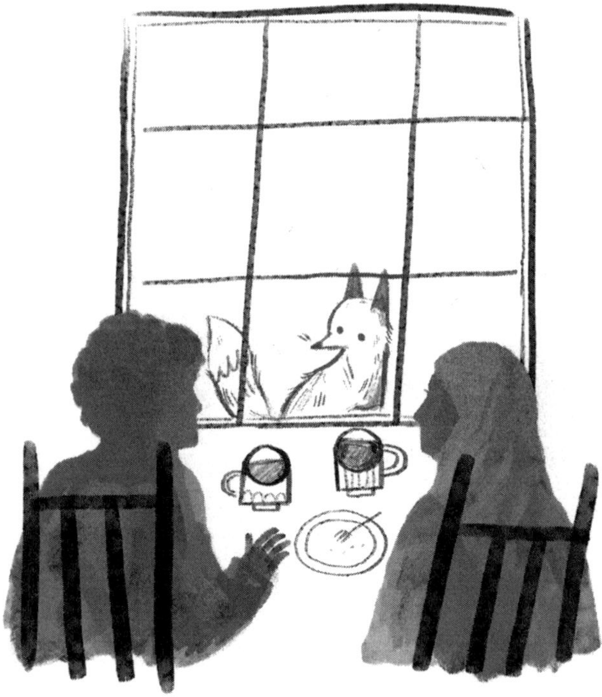

Fiction

PROXIMITY
Farhana Khalique

It's so sudden and loud that Mum pauses her knife and calls, 'Sarosh, was that from the TV or outside?'

'Outside,' I say. I'm sitting at the table in the conservatory, pretending to watch *Sunday Brunch*, but I didn't notice any lightning. Mum mutters a quick prayer, then returns to chopping vegetables. I get up and look out of the back window. There's no rain here, but I can see it bruising the sky in the distance. In the garden, the soil is sprinkled with orange peel and solar lights, which apparently deter cats from digging up coriander patches. One light is broken and the orange and plastic shards have been candied by the late snows. I can't wait till this cold snap ends.

Mum comes over to the back door with a bowl of vegetable peelings. I grab it and say, 'I'll do it.'

'Thanks, love. You staying for dinner?'

'Of course,' I say. I'm about to add why, but all I say is, 'I'll set the table later.'

'Good.' She wipes her hands on her apron, then

returns to her bubbling pot.

I slip on a pair of sandals and step outside. The air is charged with unspent rain and for a moment I just stand there and breathe. Then the cold seeps in and pricks my skin, so I hurry over to the composter and dump the waste. That's when I see the gnome, toppled over, defeated by the snow and winds. His sky blue top is chipped and cracked, and he's holding a fishing rod. Otherwise he looks like a discarded toy. I leave him fishing in the air.

Nine months ago

He was wearing a sky blue jumper when I first saw him, standing in the drizzle outside the Southbank Centre. When I went up to him, he took off his glasses and ran his fingers through his damp hair. My eyes widened; I hadn't seen him without his specs before, and I wasn't prepared for those cheekbones.

Later in the café, 'Are you sure you don't want one?' he said, pointing at his crêpe. Strawberries, chocolate, whipped cream.

'No, thanks,' I lied, too nervous to eat. I gripped my mug, sipped coffee instead.

I had downloaded the app a few months before. Having heard the success stories and having had no luck via family or friends, I'd thought: Why not? Soon, my excitement soured. Either the picture was terrible, the profile worse, or the grammar unmentionable. Half of the guys I spoke to on the phone weren't serious, or there was no chemistry in person.

So, back to (increasingly half-hearted) swiping. Then I saw Rayhan's profile. Former Fine Art student, turned graphic designer. Well travelled, well read, could even cook. Knew his Murakami from his Murata, and the difference between *there, their* and *they're*. In other words, different. *Too different?* I wondered just how glamorous me and a job in HR for the NHS could ever be. Then I thought, *sod it, won't know unless I message him*. A few text convos and a phone call later, there I was, talking about desserts and music and books with the first real-life guy I'd liked in ages. Sitting and smiling.

Now

Dinner will be a while, and Mum's taken over the TV and Dad's washing the car, so I head up to my room for more distractions. I left the window open while I was downstairs, but I close it. It was sunny this morning, now the sky glowers, unable to make up its mind. I wish it would just pour down, anything's better than this frosty gloom.

I go to my bookshelf, returning and lending things

to myself. Austen and Brontë are on the same row as Kandasamy and Vuong, there never was any order to these shelves, and I realise that most of these titles are love stories. I choose *The Haunting of Hill House*.

My guitar is where I left it so I pick that up, fingerpicking 'Time of your Life', even though my nails are too long and my fingertips are too soft. There's no room for all this in my flat, so it's nice slipping into my old skin again, just like the old days. I wonder if that's why I really came here today. To get off the rollercoaster going on out there, a brief escape to the routine and warmth of my parents' love? Or to tell them what's really been going on? What if I got their hopes up for no reason? Something pings and I glance at my phone.

I put down the guitar and grab my phone, but it's just an email, another shop having another sale. No new messages. Then I open YouTube and find the music video for 'Hide and Seek'. I binge-watched *Normal People* the other day and the soundtrack is still earworming through my head. Imogen Heap's distorted a cappella sends vibrations along my skin. Her dangly earring is so long it reaches her heart, and the butterfly on it throbs against her throat.

Six months ago

PROXIMITY

It was so humid in the butterfly house, I nearly stepped straight out. Then I saw them, pulsing around me, the ripples from their wings brushing my cheeks. I stepped forward.

It was like a cloud of never-ending confetti. As I acclimatised, I noticed one in particular, a metallic cobalt shimmer.

'Sarosh?'

I tore my eyes away. Rayhan, in a Green Day t-shirt and ripped jeans, was waiting.

We meandered around the fake tropical space, swapping stories of the hottest places we'd been to (him: Kuala Lumpur, me: Sylhet), while we dodged the speeding kids and cruising adults. I wondered why he'd picked the zoo and if he was an animal lover, even though he didn't have any pets. But we'd already done the museums and galleries, so the zoo made sense. Maybe, if all went well, we'd get a cat. Hah, Mum wouldn't like that part.

'What are you thinking about?' said Ray.

Moving in together and having a cat. 'Er,' I scanned the sky for an answer while I fanned myself with a leaflet.

'Oh, is it too hot in here, are you okay?' He came closer, searching my face.

I looked back at him, pleased he'd noticed, though

jealous of his shine-free skin. I imagined him trekking through a rainforest, his broad shoulders and long legs managing a backpack and rough terrain with ease. Unlike me, who'd already tripped once in here and could feel the sheen on my cheeks. 'Fine, thanks,' I said. 'I'm starving, though.'

He laughed. 'Let's grab lunch.'

We headed towards the exit and he parted the first door and its curtain of plastic strips for me. I saw the sign and brushed down my top first, in case I was carrying out any little friends. Ray grinned and asked me if I needed a hand. I laughed and swatted him away, then we went through the doors and emerged back out to reality.

Now

This wardrobe is a time capsule. Most of the hangers hold my Desi outfits, but there are some dresses. Long, floaty, occasiony. No occasions now, though. So here they stay, like suspended dreams.

I look but don't touch, holding them against me in the mirror of my mind. The peaches and cream one I'd have worn when we took the riverboat to Kew. The silver one for when Ray was going to take me out for my birthday. The blush pink one I was saving for Valentine's Day.

PROXIMITY

The other week on the phone, I'd suggested a Zoom date. Confused, Ray asked how that was different to any other video call, and then I frowned and changed the subject.

Either way, no point buying anything new, despite the online sales. Everything goes on sale at some point, except time.

I think about lost seasons. A lost year. An age.

I shut the wardrobe.

Three months ago

'You're so neat,' said Ray.

I looked up from our platter. He'd complimented me before of course, from my clothes, to my quirks, to my opinions. Steady sprinklings.

We were in a café in Spitalfields, just before Christmas, in a break between lockdowns. As I fiddled with the paisley scarf he'd just bought me after I admired it in the market, he added, 'Elegant.'

'Hah. I'm too clumsy.'

'I'm serious.'

Our eyes locked. In between learning more about each other and enjoying growing closer, I was hopeful that things were going in the right direction. He'd flit across my mind most hours of the day, and I'd miss the nights that we didn't speak on the phone, even if it was just about box sets and banana bread and the bloody government. He'd take the mick out of his clients and their endless list of edits, and he listened when I worried about my frontline colleagues. And when I got too fired up, he'd slip in a *so-where-d'you-wanna-go-when-this-is-all-over*? and we'd swap hazy visions of beaches and mountains and anywhere that wasn't here. I realised that it wasn't just the banter and the books and the travelling thing with him, but the noticing and the caring and the knowing exactly what to say.

But we hadn't met each other's families yet. We'd mentioned it, but not properly. It fluttered above us, whispering, *next time, next time*.

This time, his eyes were dancing. 'Very prim and proper.'

Hmm. I imagined him blindfolded. Shirtless and seated on a chair, wrists tied behind him, while I straddled him, facing him, smothering him with my proximity and control.

I held his gaze and smiled, and then slowly bit into a chip.

Now

I'm not sophisticated. Take this room; there might be a Van Gogh on the wall, but that poster's been there for a decade. My favourite chocolate is Cadbury's, my favourite crisps are ready salted, and I wouldn't know the difference between Coke and Pepsi if blindfolded.

The other day, Ray asked what Mum's favourite chocolates are, and what Ambala sweets Dad likes, and I didn't have the heart to text back the words cholesterol or diabetes. I was too busy thinking: OMG.

Whenever I'm stressed or want to treat myself, or when I'm feeling nothing or everything, it turns out I'm a simple girl; the chalky taste of Dairy Milk will do.

I'd texted back, *Truffles?*

Cool, he'd replied. Then: *Don't u wanna know what my folks like?*

Why, u planning on bringing them over?

Maybe. Lol.

When would that even be? I head over to the window again, glaring at the purpling sky. Everything's on hold, like boxed sweets on a shelf I can't reach. It's been months since I last saw Ray. We talk and video call, but what if the introductions are put off indefinitely? What if he's still talking to other girls, craving other flavours. What if I'm the only one not swiping? What if. . .?

My phone pings.

*

At dinner, there's something new.

'What's this,' I say, 'No rice?'

'It's stew, not curry, you don't need rice. But there's some bread if you're desperate, like your father.'

Dad, literally caught red-handed, squirms and then carries on dipping.

I lift a spoonful. It's not as red as what I'm used to here, but I detect paprika and coriander. I taste. It's thick, velvety and warming. 'It's good,' I say. 'What's in it, daal and–'

'Butternut squash,' says Mum. 'Got the recipe on YouTube.'

'YouTube! Last time I was here, you were asking me about WhatsApp, now you're YouTubing? I'm impressed.'

'Chup! You're not the only one learning new things under lockdown. There's lots of Desi women on there, sharing recipes.'

I laugh. Maybe I'll nick some leftovers, it would save me making anything for a couple of nights. I could pretend Mum and Dad were sitting with me while I ate.

'Have you left the cooker on?' says Dad.

'No, why–' Mum pauses.

We look up. There's a growing hissing, then drumming on the roof.

'Finally,' says Mum. 'At least now it'll feel less cold.'

I listen to the beats. I wonder what it would be like to stand outside, letting the wet and the cold and nothingness soak my bones.

'When are you lot getting vaccinated?' says Mum. 'We had our first jabs this week.'

'Soon,' I say. 'The clinicians have had theirs, but they want the other NHS departments done too, so we can fully open the building again.'

'You picked the worst time to move out. And if you're such a "key worker", then you should have just been a doctor.'

I laugh. 'At least it was before last March.'

'Hrrmm,' she says, unconvinced.

'We're very proud of you, Sarosh,' rumbles Dad.

I raise my eyebrows and then smile at him, touched. I've missed this table, its solidity.

'How's the flat?' says Mum. 'Want to take anything with you before you drive back? Seen anyone we know lately?'

'"Seen anyone?" You're the only ones I'm allowed to see right now,' I say. But I hesitate.

She notices. 'But?'

The rain hammers above, fills my ears, my brain, my skin, and then I feel something release. I put down my spoon. 'Well, I haven't seen him in person lately.'

I take a breath. 'But there's someone who wants to meet you.'

They both look up.

Not the way I'd planned to tell them, and who knows what the future holds. But in the meantime, I'll do my best, until the skies clear.

About the Authors

Marie-Claire Amuah is a British Ghanaian barrister specialising in white-collar crime. She studied English and French at the University of Nottingham before embarking on a legal career. She is also a trustee of Black Cultural Archives, a national heritage charity dedicated to collecting, preserving and celebrating the histories of African and Caribbean people in Britain. She received the John C Laurence award from the Society of Authors to support the writing of her debut novel, *One for Sorrow, Two for Joy* (Oneworld 2022). Marie-Claire was born, raised and currently lives in South London.

Santanu Bhattacharya is the author of *One Small Voice* (Penguin Fig Tree), an *Observer* Best Debut Novel for 2023. He grew up in India, and studied at the University of Oxford and the National University of Singapore. Santanu is the winner of the 2021 Mo Siewcharran Prize, the Life Writing Prize and a London Writers Award. His works have been nominated for the 4thWrite Prize, Blue

Pencil Agency First Novel Award, and Pontas & JJ Bola Emerging Writers Prize. His short fiction has appeared in Commonwealth Writers' *adda* magazine. He is a graduate of the Tin House Writers' Workshop. He currently lives in London.

Angel Dahouk is half-Lebanese, half-Madeiran, born in London. She has worked across the arts sector – from the Poetry Society to the ICA – and has written book and theatre reviews for the *Morning Star*, and poetry reviews for the *TLS* and *Poetry Review*.

Anne Elicaño-Shields is a London-based Filipino author who has just finished writing her first YA novel. Previously based in Manila, Bangkok, and Washington DC, her work is inspired by the traditional myths and urban legends of these places. Anne's writing has been published in the *How It Started* anthology, performed at the London Literature Festival at Southbank Centre, and recorded for The Classical Association's podcast. Her awards include: 2022 Creative Future Writers' Award, 2022 FABPrize Highly Commended, 2021 London Writers Awards, 2020 BESEA Free Read Award (The Literary Consultancy), and more. She lives in London with her husband and two young children. Get in touch at: anneelicano@gmail.com

Suyin Haynes is Head of Editorial at *gal-dem*, an award-winning media company dedicated to sharing the perspectives of people of colour from marginalised genders. Previously, she was a reporter for *TIME* magazine, based in both London and Hong Kong, where she covered gender, culture and underrepresented communities. Born, bred and currently living in the beloved London Borough of Bromley, 'The Steamboat' is her first published work of fiction.

Carmen Hoang works in television (not as a writer) and occasionally writes (not for television). When she does put pen to paper, she writes about British society, politics, identity, and family. Outside of that she works in scripted drama developing TV shows with a range of writers and loves playing football with her grassroots team, the Deptford Ravens.

Farhana Khalique is a writer, voiceover artist and teacher from South West London. Her writing appears in *Best Small Fictions 2022*, *100 Voices*, *This is Our Place* and more. She's been shortlisted for The Asian Writer Short Story Prize and she's a former Word Factory Apprentice. Farhana is also a submissions editor at *SmokeLong Quarterly*, a fiction editor at *Litro*, and has taught workshops with Flash Fiction Festival, Crow Collective, Dahlia Publishing and more. Find Farhana @HanaKhalique or at: farhanakhalique.com

Yuebai Liu is a researcher working with brands and organisations to help them understand the complex systems we live in. She is also a non-fiction writer, and her writing explores themes of identity, migration and belonging through diasporic experiences. Yuebai has been published in *Slate Magazine*, *Al Jazeera*, *Roads & Kingdoms*, *Mail & Guardian* and *TechNode*.

Lola Pereira is a queer British-Nigerian writer. Her writing tells tales of strong family connections and the magic that strings love and care between generations. She was a winner of TLC's 2022 Michael Langan LGBTQ+ Free Reads for her novel manuscript. Lola lives in London, pondering the ending of her first novel.

Kari Pindoria is a writer from London. She often daydreams all day and drinks too much tea. Her poetry has been previously published in *Ink, Sweat and Tears* and *Unbroken Journal*. She is a part of the 2022-23 Roundhouse Poetry Collective.

Priscilla Yeung is a bi-lingual novelist and writer from Hong Kong, based in London. She is currently reading an MA in Creative Writing at City, University of London. Her writing explores the diasporic experience and mental health of urban dwellers. Her work appears in *Literally Stories*, the University of Oxford's *Torch* magazine, *Antithesis* and elsewhere. She is long-listed for the 2023 Book Edit Prize. Find Priscilla @midoribythesea, or at: priscillayeung.com.

TOKEN

TOKEN is a literature and arts print magazine that features written pieces and artwork by underrepresented artists and writers. The first issue launched in May 2017. It is created, edited and designed by Sara Jafari. The name comes from the experience of tokenism that underrepresented groups often face; the magazine aims to push against this and more accurately represent the world we all live in.

Tales from the City is TOKEN'S first book.

tokenmagazine.co.uk

Deptford Literature Festival

Deptford Literature Festival celebrates the diversity and creativity of Deptford and Lewisham through stories, words and performance. It is run by Spread the Word in collaboration with creative producer Tom MacAndrew, and funded by Arts Council England, with support from The Albany and Deptford Lounge. The festival takes place in locations across Deptford and features local literary talent and organisations. It explores what literature means to us in South East London, and includes a programme of workshops, talks, walks, readings and performances. It aims to offer something for everyone; whether you're an experienced reader or writer, or just want to have a go.

deptfordliteraturefestival.com

Tom MacAndrew is a freelance producer specialising in poetry, spoken word and live literature. He has produced work for National Poetry Day, Penned in the Margins, BBC Radio 4 and BBC Arts; and developed and toured shows by poets Joelle Taylor, Joshua Idehen, Francesca Beard and John Hegley. He is the producer of the regular poetry series Out-Spoken at Southbank Centre and the Bedtime Stories for the End of the World podcast series, as well as the editor of the accompanying illustrated book, published by Studio Press.

tommacandrew.com

Spread the Word has a national and international reputation for initiating change-making research and developing programmes for writers that have equity and social justice at their heart. In 2015 it launched, Writing the Future: Black and Asian Writers and Publishers in the UK Market Place. In 2020 it launched Rethinking 'Diversity' in Publishing by Dr Anamik Saha and Dr Sandra van Lente, Goldsmiths, University of London, in partnership with The Bookseller and Words of Colour. Spread the Word's programmes in addition to Deptford Literature Festival include the London Writers Awards, CRIPtic x Spread the Word and Wellcome Collection x Spread the Word Writing Awards.

spreadtheword.org.uk